# FLIP AND GROW RICH

## THE HEART AND MIND OF REAL ESTATE INVESTING

# ARMANDO MONTELONGO

### WITH HELEN KAIAO CHANG

**www.armandocoaching.com**
**1-800-771-6202 ext 4001**

ISBN: 978-0-9795960-0-1

Printed in the United States of America

First Edition

*This book is dedicated to those who believe
that **now** is a good time to make a change.*

# Contents

Introduction . . . . . . . . . . . . . . . . . . . . . . . . . . . . . . . . . . . . . . . . . . . 1
*How to Read This Book for the Richest Experience*

## The Heart of Real Estate Investing
Follow Armando's Journey to Success

Chapter 1    **America's Biggest Flipper** . . . . . . . . . . . . . . . . . . . . . . 4
*If My Dreams Can Come True, So Can Yours*

            • A Boy's Dream
            • Dreams Come True
            • A Change in Beliefs
            • The Cornerstone of Wealth
            • True Wealth

Chapter 2    **A Day in the Life** . . . . . . . . . . . . . . . . . . . . . . . . . . . . . 12
*My Schedule of Work, Family and Fun*

            • My Life
            • A Typical Day
            • Next Level

Chapter 3    **Growing Up** . . . . . . . . . . . . . . . . . . . . . . . . . . . . . . . . 26
*Choosing My Beliefs*

            • Honesty and Hard Work
            • Love of Learning
            • Personal Economies
            • Family Rebel

Chapter 4    **How I Met Veronica** . . . . . . . . . . . . . . . . . . . . . . . . 38
*Listening to My Dreams*

            • California Party
            • Donut Shops
            • Knock on the Door
            • Together

# The Mind of Real Estate Investing

Learn Armando's Secrets to Success

Chapter A  **How Flipping Houses Can Change Your Life**....5
Achieve Wealth and Freedom by Investing in Real Estate
- Wealth
- Freedom
- Lifestyle
- Any Age
- Write Your Own Paycheck

Chapter B  **Overcome Your Biggest Obstacles** ...........13
Why You, Too, Can Flip Houses
- Inspired Fans
- Where to Get Money
- Where to Find Good Deals
- How to Do Your First Flip
- How to Flip Houses in Your Market
- If You Don't Have Business Experience
- How to Overcome Fear
- How to Get Started

Chapter C  **Know Your Values** .........................27
Building the Mental Foundation
- Honesty
- Integrity
- More Money
- Smart Work
- The Gift of Problems
- Money as a Positive Force

Chapter 5     **No Money, No Credit, Massive Debt** . . . . . . . . . . . . 50
*How I Started with Nothing*

> • My Greatest Inspiration
> • Blood Complications
> • The Worst Day of My Life
> • Medical Debt
> • Food Stamps
> • Foreclosure
> • Living in a Garage
> • The Turning Point

Chapter 6     **Return to San Antonio** . . . . . . . . . . . . . . . . . . . . . . . . 70
*My Promise to Veronica*

> • The Long Drive
> • Promise to Veronica
> • Last Tank of Gas
> • The Biggest Regret
> • A Husband's Motivation
> • Bad Economy
> • Creating My Assets List
> • Assuming Success

Chapter 7     **My First Deal** . . . . . . . . . . . . . . . . . . . . . . . . . . . . . 86
*Taking Action*

> • Chasing Fire Trucks
> • Insurance Agent's Call
> • Lisa's Story
> • Finding the Money
> • Selling the Property

Chapter 8     **The Next Deal** . . . . . . . . . . . . . . . . . . . . . . . . . . . . 102
*Learning from Lawyers*

> • Looking for Deals
> • Solving Attorneys' Problems
> • The Expert Witness Deal
> • Splitting Costs

Chapter D    **Your Money Mentors** . . . . . . . . . . . . . . . . . . . . . . 39
Business Masters Can Help Fuel Your Success
      • Mentors
      • Environment of Empowerment
      • Continuous Learning
      • Your Inner Intelligence

Chapter E    **Your Money Mind** . . . . . . . . . . . . . . . . . . . . . . . . . .53
Success Begins with Your Thoughts
      • Limitations
      • Myths and Facts
      • Analysis Paralysis
      • Critical Moment
      • Know Your "Why"
      • Assets List
      • Daily Actions
      • Make Mistakes

Chapter F    **Make Money in Any Market** . . . . . . . . . . . . . . . . .73
Deals Dictate Success, Whether the Market is Up, Down or Flat
      • Flip in Any Market
      • Buy a Property, Not a Market
      • Falling Markets
      • Flat Markets
      • Rising Markets
      • Rolling Strategies

Chapter G    **How to Find Deals** . . . . . . . . . . . . . . . . . . . . . . . .85
Solving Homeowners' Problems First
      • Deals Before Money
      • Find Motivated Sellers
      • How to Negotiate with Homeowners
      • WIIFM Radio

Chapter H    **Deals from Attorneys** . . . . . . . . . . . . . . . . . . . . . .107
Buying Homes from Homeowners with Insurance Claims
      • Find Insurance Lawyers
      • Why Homeowners Sue
      • How Settlements Work
      • The Expert Witness' Role
      • How Homeowners Can Profit
      • How Homeowners Use Settlements
      • Sample Letter to Lawyer

Chapter 9      **Honing My Skills** . . . . . . . . . . . . . . . . . . . . . . . . . . .116
               *The Basics of My Business*

                      • Learning Experiences
                      • Jail and Bail
                      • Show Me the Money
                      • Mastermind Group
                      • The New Goal

Chapter 10     **Multimillionaire Mentors** . . . . . . . . . . . . . . . . . . . . .132
               *Strategies for Long-Term Wealth*

                      • Chasing Multimillionaires
                      • The Doctor Investor
                      • Speed of Cash Theory
                      • My $60,000 Mistake

Chapter 11     **Learning to Sell** . . . . . . . . . . . . . . . . . . . . . . . . . . . . .148
               *Creating Excited Buyers and Sellers*

                      • Selling By Auction
                      • Owner-Financed Deals
                      • No Junk Fees
                      • Expanding My Team
                      • Following My Instincts

Chapter 12     **Finding Balance** . . . . . . . . . . . . . . . . . . . . . . . . . . . . .160
               *Remembering My "Why"*

                      • Late Dinner Talks
                      • What Veronica Needed
                      • Flipping from Happiness

Chapter I      **More Ways to Find Deals** ................. 125
Create a System for Leads
- Business Systems
- Foreclosures
- Short Sales
- REO Real Estate Agents
- Bail Bondsmen
- Finding Systems

Chapter J      **Where to Find Money** ..................... 137
Tap into an Abundance of Investment Money
- The Speed of Cash at Work
- How Much to Pay
- The 70 Percent Rule
- Hard-Money Lenders
- Private Investors
- Partners
- Funding Systems

Chapter K      **Ways to Sell** ............................ 151
Realize Profits with an Array of Options
- Plan Your Exits
- Wider Range of Buyers
- Strategies for Cash Flow
- Real Estate Agents
- Auctions
- Owner Financing
- Lease Options
- Wholesaling
- Selling to Landlords
- Selling Systems
- Marketing Systems

Chapter L      **True Wealth** ............................ 173
Remember Your "Why"
- Definition of Wealth
- Create Balance
- Clean Your Garage
- Schedule Activities
- Part-Time Investing

Chapter 13    **Building Systems** . . . . . . . . . . . . . . . . . . . . . . . . . . . . 176
*Work Less and Earn More*

- Ideal Scenario
- The Employee Mistake
- Duplicating Myself
- Challenges
- Systems
- Less Time, More Money

Chapter 14    **Deals Everywhere** . . . . . . . . . . . . . . . . . . . . . . . . . . . 192
*My Business Overflows with Leads*

- Rolling with Deals
- The House with Goats and Sheep
- The No-Mold Short Sale
- The Partnership Flip
- The Multi-House Package
- The Fishing Guy's Retreat

Chapter 15    **Enjoying the Wealth** . . . . . . . . . . . . . . . . . . . . . . . . 214
*Sharing My Abundance*

- Buying Whatever I Want
- Lifestyle of Athletes
- Vacations
- Thanking My Family
- Our Dream Home
- I Had Arrived

Chapter 16    **Landing the TV Show** . . . . . . . . . . . . . . . . . . . . . . 226
*Daring to Dream Big*

- Pipe Dream
- The Application
- The Producer Flies Out
- The Wait
- The Stand-In Actor's House
- The Launch Party
- Mondo Man's Night

Chapter M     **How to Fix** . . . . . . . . . . . . . . . . . . . . . . . . . . . . . . . . . . . .181
              Use Systems to Streamline Construction
                   • Fix Houses for Maximum Profit
                   • Cookie-Cutter Rules
                   • Seven Rules to Maximize Profits
                   • Assessing Repairs
                   • Dealing with Animal Odors
                   • Replace Yourself
                   • Paperwork Systems
                   • How to Manage Contractors
                   • Contractor Paperwork

Chapter N     **Mentoring Others** . . . . . . . . . . . . . . . . . . . . . . . . . .197
              How These Methods Can Work for Anybody
                   • Coaching Students
                   • Theresa – In Debt and Pregnant
                   • Raymond – Paying Off the IRS
                   • Larry – The 72-Year-Old Retiree
                   • The Rewards

Chapter O     **How to Get Rich** . . . . . . . . . . . . . . . . . . . . . . . . . . . . .215
              Keep Your Fountain of Wealth Flowing
                   • How Much to Invest
                   • Investments Before Luxury
                   • Five Levels of Earning Income
                   • Use Money to Make Money
                   • How to Manage Your Profits
                   • When to Quit Your Job
                   • The Path to True Wealth
                   • The Path to True Lifestyle

Chapter P     **Set Your Goals** . . . . . . . . . . . . . . . . . . . . . . . . . . . . .235
              You Can Achieve Your Biggest Dreams
                   • Follow Your Dreams
                   • Write Down Your Goals
                   • Business Checkups
                   • Face Your Fears
                   • Have Fun!

Chapter 17    **The First Season** . . . . . . . . . . . . . . . . . . . . . . . . . . . . . . .248
*Solving People's Problems – Even on Television*

  • Love Us or Hate Us
  • Ratings Skyrocket
  • Shouting from the Back Room
  • A Regular Guy
  • Business Heats Up
  • Stress Builds
  • Rancho Montelongo
  • Another TV Contract

Chapter 18    **The Second Season** . . . . . . . . . . . . . . . . . . . . . . . . .270
*Expanding My Business Scope*

  • Highest Ratings
  • Remembering My Promise
  • The Cat House
  • A Family Split
  • Veronica's Deal
  • Veronica's Promotion
  • Rental and Commercial Deals
  • Flipping in Other Markets
  • New Mentors
  • City Benefits

Chapter 19    **Sharing the Knowledge** . . . . . . . . . . . . . . . . . . . . . . .296
*Expanding My "Why"*

  • The Need to Serve
  • My Everyday System
  • Future Goals
  • New Dreams

Chapter Q    **How to Save on Taxes** .......................251
Earn a Bundle by Understanding Legal Structures
• Your Rights
• Flip Your Own House
• How to Live in Your House for Free
• More Savings
• Another Way to Save on Taxes
• Legal Entities
• Write Off Vacations

Chapter R    **Other Investments** ..........................269
Building Long-Term Wealth
• Business Partners
• Focus
• Downside of Wealth
• Now Cash vs. Future Cash
• Rental and Commercial Properties
• International Markets
• Larger Benefits

Chapter S    **How You Can Start Flipping** ................287
Create a New Future
• Find a Mentor
• Learn from the Best
• Proven Systems
• Serve Yourself
• Share the Knowledge
• Change Your Future
• How You Can Learn

Acknowledgements ...........................................303
About the Authors ..........................................307
Index ......................................................308
Flip and Grow Rich Products ................................316
Flip and Grow Rich Coaching ................................318
Flip and Grow Rich Workshops................................319

# Introduction

*How to Read This Book for the Richest Experience*

Congratulations on picking up this book. It could be your first step to achieving wealth, freedom and a great lifestyle.

It is my goal to inspire you through my real life story as well as teach you real world strategies about how to flip houses and grow rich.

Investing requires passion and knowledge. You cannot have success without inspiration, and you cannot turn inspiration into profits if you do not have a business system.

That's why this book is set up to appeal to both.

The left side of the book tells you my personal story — how I started from nothing and grew into a multimillionaire real estate investor. You share in the hope, despair, fear and excitement I have experienced on my road to success.

The right side of the book explains how to succeed in real estate investing — how to condition your mind for success, find hot deals, secure money, manage contractors, reinvest profits and enjoy true wealth. You learn the secrets to my business without going through the school of hard knocks.

Each chapter is complete. You can jump around and read the sections that seem most relevant at the moment. Let's say you are wondering about how to find money. You can skip ahead to that chapter and learn that first, then circle back and read other parts later.

Or, you might want to read my entire personal story first and then read all of the explanations to understand more about the business.

Some names have been changed. But all the deals are real.

As I climbed the ladder of success, I was fortunate enough to find millionaire mentors who helped me along the way. Without these mentors, I would have lost money, time and hope. Without mentors, I would not have accomplished my goals or dreams. These mentors helped me become a millionaire within one year and a multimillionaire today.

That is why I am happy to share my secrets – to help others coming up behind me. If at any point you would like to use my coaches as a resource, feel free to call: 1-800-771-6202 x 4001.

Ultimately, I hope this book will help you achieve your life dreams. No matter how big your dreams may seem, they can come true. They did for me.

# Chapter 1

## America's Biggest Flipper
### *If My Dreams Can Come True, So Can Yours*

- **A Boy's Dream**
- **Dreams Come True**
- **A Change in Beliefs**
- **The Cornerstone of Wealth**
- **True Wealth**

## A Boy's Dream

I have dreams, just like you do. My question for you is this: have you given up on those dreams?

When I was a boy, I dreamed of being a great businessman. I would be rich, have a beautiful wife, head a great family, live in an awesome house, travel the world and be known by millions.

I always had that dream, but at times in my life I didn't think it was possible. That's when I lived in a garage, was $50,000 in debt, had no money, horrible credit, and relied on food stamps to support my wife and son.

# Chapter A

## How Flipping Houses Can Change Your Life
Achieve Wealth and Freedom by Investing in Real Estate

- **Wealth**
- **Freedom**
- **Lifestyle**
- **Any Age**
- **Write Your Own Paycheck**

### Wealth

In America, 97 percent of all self-made millionaires created their fortune through real estate, according to *Fortune* magazine. I applaud you for picking up this book, because you now are on the right track to calling your own shots in life.

Real estate wealth is not dependent on any market. In real estate, people can make money whether the market is bad, flat or good. It is possible to make money in any market.

Flipping houses is great, because if you need a cash infusion within a few months, rather than waiting to make a couple hundred dollars, you can make between $20,000 and $80,000 on one flip. You can use this not only to support yourself, but also to stash away money and build your cash reserves.

## Dreams Come True

But dreams do come true. They have for me. Today, I am one of the largest house-flipping investors in America. I am able to consistently flip 25 to 30 houses a month. My corporation controls dozens of rental properties, including single-family residences, apartment buildings and commercial properties.

I am married to the woman of my dreams. She is my partner in life and the vice president of our business. Our son is the light of our lives. We go on vacation once every three months, taking seven to 10 days off at a time. Our family has traveled to isolated beach resorts in Mexico. We have driven across the U.S. and visited places my son loves — Disneyland, Six Flags and Knott's Berry Farm. The business legitimately pays for most of these travel expenses through tax write-offs.

And we have a reality-TV show, "Flip This House," which airs on the A&E cable channel. It is the highest-rated house-flipping show on air. It has spawned other house-rehabbing shows, as well as spoofs.

To many people, my life would seem like a dream. No matter how real my dreams are now, I started in a situation that most people would consider a downright nightmare. However, I found a way to make my dreams come true and it is my intention to help you make your dreams come true as well.

## A Change in Beliefs

I am not that different from you. The main thing I did was to change my beliefs and take action. Have I made lots of mistakes? Sure. I have been called all kinds of names – asshole, idiot, loser. Sometimes, I even thought those things about myself.

Flipping houses allows you to pay off old debt and create financial security. You create financial freedom, which means you can buy what you want when you want. That is why flipping houses is the best way to start your real estate career. Real estate is simple, understandable and tangible.

## Freedom

The greatest movies in the world are about freedom – freedom from evil, freedom to love, freedom to do as you please. One of the most treasured things that we have in this world is freedom.

Real estate investing can give you freedom. Flipping houses can give you the time and space to do what you want.

Do you feel burdened by any of the following?

- huge debt
- medical bills
- house payments
- car payments
- small paychecks
- overbearing boss
- lack of personal time

Flipping houses can give you the opportunity to turn your situation around.

But I never stopped improving, moving forward and following my dreams. I trusted my gut instinct that I could live a phenomenal life. I acted, despite fear. You can, too.

When I was at my lowest point, I made a promise to my wife, Veronica, that if we ever became successful, we would share it with other people. I promised that if I accomplished my dreams, I would share my secrets with the world. I have kept that promise. I have taught my methods to our family, community, investors in San Antonio, millions of TV fans and now you.

I hope that by reading my story, you will be inspired to go after your dreams. Whatever your circumstances, you can find a way to achieve your life goals. The only thing stopping you is between your ears. The one thing that made a difference is I changed my beliefs. Now, I will show you how to change your beliefs in order to achieve greater success.

### The Cornerstone of Wealth

For me, the way to fulfill my dreams was through real estate. My path to success was through building a real estate flipping machine. It's a business that has helped my family, as well as thousands of other people. Ultimately, it's a people business. The more I solve other people's problems, the more I am rewarded.

Real estate is the cornerstone of wealth in America. According to *Fortune* magazine, 97 percent of all self-made millionaires became rich through real estate.

### True Wealth

I am certain that you can strip me of all my money, property and assets, close my bank account and cut up my credit cards, fly me

### Lifestyle

Real estate investing can give you the lifestyle you desire, so that you have more time and money to:

- spend time with your loved ones
- go on vacations
- buy your dream home
- save for the future
- create a legacy for your family
- live your dream life

Flipping houses allows you to create the lifestyle you want. Lifestyle is having not only the money, but the time to do the things you want to do. You see, in life, most people are time-broke or money-broke or both. And flipping real estate can remedy both of those things for you, if that is your desire.

### Any Age

A 60-year-old man once asked me, "Is it too late for me to get into real estate?"

My response was, "You know what? In five years, you are going to be five years older anyway. So why not be five years older with money in your pocket?"

It's never too late or too early to get into real estate, and if you're looking to turn your life around and create wealth, flipping houses is the way to do it.

to any market in America with $200 to my name, and I can make $1 million in a year.

Does $1 million make me wealthy? No. Does the infinite belief that I can make $1 million – under any circumstance in any environment – make me wealthy? Absolutely!

Even as we grow as individuals, Veronica and I will always flip houses, because it is one of the greatest and fastest wealth generators known to mankind.

**Write Your Own Paycheck**

Peace of mind comes from knowing that you can take care of your family, and that your loved ones can take care of themselves. I know that if anything ever happened to me, my wife, Veronica, would be able to support herself and our son very easily by flipping houses.

A lot of people look for security from employers and paychecks. But to me, that is the scariest thought in the world – that someone else's signature on a piece of paper determines my future for next week or how I'm going to meet my monthly bills. The only way to ensure true financial security and freedom is to be able to sign your own paychecks.

If you're a single parent, a married couple, fresh out of school, a senior citizen, a wife whose husband is a slave to his employer, a soccer mom, a man who is tired of his job or simply looking for a way to ensure financial security, you can change your future. You do not have to be destined for a life of poverty or just getting by. You can change and take control of your financial destiny.

Educate yourself and get in the game of flipping houses. It's a game anyone can play and win.

# Chapter 2

## A Day in the Life
### *My Schedule of Work, Family and Fun*

- **My Life**
- **A Typical Day**
- **Next Level**

## My Life

Before you read about my life, I want to make it clear that you do not have to run crazy the way I do. It does not have to take this much work to be successful. I only live and work the way I do, because I love it. At the same time, I created a system of success for you, so that you can live life on your terms and not have to work long and ridiculous hours.

I run on full throttle. I typically work 15-hour days. I have five businesses. I field close to 100 phone calls a day, mostly involving deals. I receive leads for houses every day. I am invited to do public speaking, as well as do television and radio interviews every day. I get e-mails from thousands of fans every day. My house flipping business continues to thrive.

I also have a TV show, Web business, coaching business and training products. No one has to operate like this. But I do it because I enjoy it.

My life is very busy, but I work for myself. I really don't follow a strict schedule. Some days I get up at 4 a.m. and some days I get up at 9 a.m.

# Chapter B

## Overcome Your Biggest Obstacles
Why You, Too, Can Flip Houses

- **Inspired Fans**
- **Where to Get Money**
- **Where to Find Good Deals**
- **How to Do Your First Flip**
- **How to Flip Houses in Your Market**
- **If You Don't Have Business Experience**
- **How to Overcome Fear**
- **How to Get Started**

### Inspired Fans

Since launching our TV show, "Flip This House," in 2006, thousands of people have e-mailed and called, saying, "Armando, this show has inspired me to get into real estate." Then they ask questions like, "How do I do it?" "How do I find that first house?" or "How do I get the money?"

I realized there is a need for me to teach people about how I flip houses, and it was time for me to keep a promise I had made to my wife to teach other people how to be successful.

Some weeks, I might work on a Sunday and go whitewater
rafting with my son on Tuesday. But generally, I work 15-hour days.


**A Typical Day**

This is what my typical day looks like:

6:30 a.m.: WAKE UP. I wake up and go to the gym.

7:15 – 8 a.m.: EXERCISE. I work out. I check-in regularly with a
fitness trainer, though my body is a work in progress.

8:30 – 9 a.m.: SCAN FOR DEALS. I'm back at home. I eat
breakfast prepared by our house assistant. While eating, I check my
e-mail. I search for deals that have rolled in.

I receive up to 30 leads a day. Realtors, competitors, fans and sources
e-mail me deals. I read the numbers on the deals and assess potential. I
can tell within a minute whether it's worth going after.

Here's how I analyze deals. First, I check if the seller is motivated.
A motivated seller means there's a better opportunity for a good
price. Next, I look at pictures, if there are any. I check out the
condition of the house – is it in good or poor shape? The worse the
condition, the greater the opportunity for turning a big profit. Then
I run the numbers. Is the asking price below the market value? This
quick information tells me if this is a deal I want to do. If a seller is
motivated, the house needs work and the price is below market, then I
analyze the numbers further for profit potential.

When I find a promising deal, I send it via e-mail to my buyer. I send
her about seven or eight deals a day. My buyer knows my system. She
looks through the multiple-listing service, or MLS, used by real estate

I actually resisted doing it at first, because I was so involved with my company. But later I thought, "I am one of the biggest house flippers in the country. I know how to do it. It is now time to step up to the plate and teach people how I do what I do every day."

When it came to flipping real estate, people asked thousands of questions. But all the questions boiled down to several basic concerns, all related to these challenges:

How can I flip houses if I have:

- no money

- no credit

- no business experience

- no construction experience

And I am stuck in:

- a slow market

- my own fear

Most people have one or two of the above six challenges.

But when I began flipping, I had all six. So if I could flip houses with all six obstacles at one time, you can flip with only a few of these challenges. In fact, you can flip houses with all six of them.

agents to find comparable homes that have sold in the area. She checks to see if the properties I have sent are good deals.

As soon as my buyer gets a property under contract, she brings it to me for review and final stamp of approval. My buyer is a scout who earns an assignment fee for every property she puts under contract. She gets paid when the deal closes. I rarely need to search for deals anymore.

Sometimes, I just wholesale a property to other flippers. Let's say I charge another flipper $7,000 for an assignment fee. I'll take $3,500 and give the buyer $3,500.

9 a.m.: CHECK IN WITH MY BUSINESS TEAM. I start fielding phone calls. On an average day, I might field up to 100 phone calls – from sellers, real estate agents, lenders, project managers, my coaching company, TV production crew, IT staff, attorneys, the CPA, the house manager, office manager, the press and my wife, Veronica.

About 90 percent of my business is done by phone. The bulk of my phone calls are for making deals – whether that means buying a house, selling a house, planning a new coaching program or creating a Web site product. It's fun and it keeps my edge sharp.

When I talk to my accountant or lawyer, it is about reviewing paperwork on complex deals. If I'm buying an apartment building or working with new lenders, they review everything to make sure it's all square. I don't have them deal with average cookie-cutter flips.

I also call my project manager to check on the progress of our rehab houses. My project manager typically oversees around 10 properties at any given time. He does not manage houses that are already on the market. We might talk for 30 minutes on any given day.

When I talk to my project manager early in the week, typically I will

Even for people who do have money to invest, the question they ask is: "How do I maximize my money and investments?"

If you have money and you want to learn how to explode your wealth, then this book will absolutely help you do that. In fact, I believe that by working with my system, you will make your wealth grow exponentially.

Here's a quick summary of how to overcome these biggest obstacles.

The following chapters explain each of these points in detail.

### Where to Get Money

Getting the money comes after finding the deal. First you get the deal. Then you get the money. Money follows deals.

The truth is that everywhere you look there's money. The streets of America are paved with gold. Everywhere. There are millions of dollars.

Why is there so much money? Because companies and private investors want to lend money to people who know how to make money. They would rather give it to a rehabber, or flipper, than put it in a bank offering low interest rates.

### Where to Find Good Deals

First, you have to get past the mental block that there are no good deals. You must understand that it's a myth. Another

ask what he completed at the end of last week and what his goals are for the coming week. He tells me what he plans to accomplish, and then I'll tell him what I would like accomplished. Usually, my goals are much more aggressive than his. I'll give him deadlines for completion.

For example, my project manager might be having trouble getting a contractor to show up and complete a job. I will ask why it's not done yet, and my project manager will tell me the contractor's reasons, which to me equal nothing but excuses. So I say that unless it's a massive medical emergency or weather condition, if the guy does not show up for three days, go ahead and fire him. That's why we have an iron-clad contractor's agreement.

One day, I had a conversation with my project manager about a problem. The contractor was taking too long to paint the house, and my project manager did not know what to do. I coached him on how to handle it. I said that people always remember what's in it for them. If my project manager reminds the contractor that the sooner he finishes, the sooner he will get paid, that will motivate him. It just comes from experience working with contractors.

I set only two kinds of goals for my project manager – money and time. Money goals are budgets. Time goals are deadlines. Let's say I wanted a house completed within three weeks and it's not done. I find out why and create a new deadline.

Maybe three major things are not complete – plumbing fixtures, exterior siding and exterior paint. Rather than lumping them together as one large goal, I break it down to make it easier mentally. So I might say all the plumbing fixtures need to be done by Wednesday; all the siding needs to be installed by Friday; and all the painting completed by Sunday.

By breaking down the deadlines, my project manager has smaller goals to manage. It takes pressure off and helps him figure out new ways to run the job.

myth is "It's hard to make money."

Start believing that it's easy to make money. I believe you should walk into every deal thinking that deals are easy to find. There are hundreds of thousands of houses with adjustable-rate mortgages and balloon notes. Foreclosures are skyrocketing and will continue to climb, which means that there are opportunities everywhere.

Educate yourself on where to find the deals. Once you know how, it's easy to find deals. Once you find deals, you can teach yourself about a new world of investment possibilities.

### How to Do Your First Flip

Here's your order of action:

1. EDUCATION – Get an education.

2. DEAL – Get the deal. The deal always comes before the money.

3. MONEY – Get the money. You've found the right type of deal that the right type of lender wants.

4. CONSTRUCTION – Get the contractor. Contractors are easy to find and more willing to work with you than you might think. Education will teach you how to handle your contractors.

5. EXIT – Figure out your sales or exit strategy. You can exit the house through a real estate agent, auction or another way. I have six different strategies for how to sell the house.

**10 a.m.: DEVELOP PROJECTS.** I call my writer, Helen, and we'll discuss a plan of action for our current project. We might also talk about the next project I am developing to teach people how to make money — through books, e-books or real estate courses.

**10:30 – 11:30 a.m.: UPDATE MY FANS.** I get on the computer and send an e-mail blast to my students and fan base. I do this about three times a week. I give updates on my day-to-day activities, tips for flipping houses, topics for upcoming Webinars or new things happening with Veronica, my son, Mondo Man, and me.

**11:30 a.m.: PLAN EVENTS.** I call Joe at my coaching company. I ask him to update me on any new students, plans, seminars or events.

**12:30 – 1 p.m.: HIGH-SPEED LUNCH.** I have lunch alone or with Veronica at the office, house or on the road.

**1:30 – 3:30 p.m.: CHECK PROPERTIES.** I drive over to check on one or two properties. The TV film crew usually follows me on these visits.

Even though I'm not as involved in day-to-day activities anymore, I still enjoy seeing what's going on with our rehab houses. I might run through a few things with my project manager to clear obstacles and help him grow as a project manager. This is not something I have to do; it's something I enjoy doing.

Sometimes personal interaction can make all the difference. If there's an issue we could not resolve on the phone, I might interact with the project manager and the contractor. But mostly, I like to let my project manager get the job done, so the contractor does not try to go around him and renegotiate with me.

For instance, on one house the project manager said the roof was OK, but the contractor insisted that it needed replacing. I reviewed my original notes on the property, and then went out to see if we

### If You Don't Have Business Experience

Perfect. You won't have any preconceived ideas. People with less business experience see things with a fresh pair of eyes.

When you learn from someone who knows what they are doing, you tend to be more humble. When you get educated, you will absorb ideas like a sponge. You will learn the things you need to know.

The flipping business does not require inventory, machines, employees, startup capital or even business experience. It's an anti-business business. It only takes knowledge.

### How to Overcome Fear

The truth is, everyone is afraid. If you just focus on what you're afraid of, that's what you will face. If you consistently focus on your dreams, you will succeed.

The vast majority of successful people started with no money and no credit. They did not inherit wealth, receive it as a gift or win the lottery. They acquired wealth the way I did – with no money, no credit and no business experience.

The vast majority of successful people overcame their fear of failure because they realized that doing nothing was ultimate failure. The ability to never give up is what creates ultimate success.

7:30 p.m.: NEW PROJECTS. Evenings are my creative time. This is when I think about new projects, explore new ideas or look for new deals. I might jump back on the computer and see what I can find.

I use this time to think about how to grow my businesses and product lines, how to deal with business partners, or I do a few real estate deals online. Again, it's not work that I have to do. It's work that I enjoy doing.

Veronica and I typically go out one night a week – either to a party or on a date. We get invited to tons of parties and social events, but we keep it to a minimum because even though we're in the public eye, we still like to be private. We like having time at home to decompress, and we like spending time with Mondo Man.

## Next Level

I feel that I have achieved many of my dreams. And I am going to the next level of helping others make their dreams come true.

My story will show you how I got to where I am today.

**How to Get Started**

By reading this book, you will get a glimpse into my world and learn the key principles and methods that I use every day.

Beyond that, the best way to get started is to call my personally trained coaches. Bar none, this is the best way to launch your investing career. You'll learn from the best so that you can become the best.

Visit www.armandocoaching.com or
call 1-800-771-6202 x 4001.

# Chapter 3

## Growing Up
*Choosing My Beliefs*

- **Honesty and Hard Work**
- **Love of Learning**
- **Personal Economies**
- **Family Rebel**

## Honesty and Hard Work

When I was a baby, my mother would play with me and play with me and play with me, just to get me to make noise. She said I was a very quiet baby. However, once I started talking, she said, I never stopped. I have been talking ever since.

I was born in San Antonio in 1970. I grew up in a family of eight children. I was the seventh. When you're the seventh of eight children, everyone picks on you. They don't pick on the baby, the smallest one. So I learned the art of verbal self-defense early on. I had a lot of weaknesses, but one thing I became great at was speaking.

My dad is a Mexican American from San Antonio. My mom is an Irish American from Tennessee. They met at an ice cream shop. She was 17 and he was 24. My dad walked in with his buddies, saw her and

# Chapter C

## Know Your Values
Building the Mental Foundation

- **Honesty**
- **Integrity**
- **More Money**
- **Smart Work**
- **The Gift of Problems**
- **Money as a Positive Force**

### Honesty

Many people believe that you have to be cunning, dishonest or swindle people to make money. This is a popular myth that actually prevents good people from making lots of money. The truth is this: Lying, stealing and cheating in business may create short-term success, but it will bring long-term downfall.

I have had the privilege of being raised by honest parents and meeting people who live life with high values and standards. That laid a foundation for me to be honest and work with integrity.

The biggest thing in business is doing what you say you're going to do, because that builds your reputation. If you have a

said, "That is the most beautiful woman I have ever seen. I am going to marry her." They have been married for more than 50 years.

When I was little, my dad was a football coach and my mom stayed at home with us kids. My dad never told a lie. He is a phenomenally honest man. I learned from him the value of honesty. My mom was an extremely dedicated individual. Raising eight children, she was always busy, always working. She didn't have much time to rest. I learned from her the importance of hard work. She taught me not to be lazy.

My parents also had the ability to keep our family together. I had a very stable childhood. We lived in the same house for more than 18 years. We lived in a middle-class neighborhood with middle-class friends in San Antonio. It is a fairly big city with lots of outlying suburbs, located pretty much in the middle of Texas.

## Love of Learning

Growing up, I always liked strange facts. I loved reading *Ripley's Believe It or Not!* and *The Guinness Book of World Records*. I loved to obtain information. That catapulted me into reading hundreds of books.

I would tell my mom stuff that I learned from Ripley's. I'd say things like, "Did you know that comedian Charlie Chaplin once entered a Charlie Chaplin look-alike contest — and lost?"

As a boy, I would read late into the night. When my parents told me go to bed, I would pull out a Hardy Boys mystery book and turn the flashlight on under the covers. I couldn't put the books down.

When I grew up, I continued to love learning. When I started my career, I read hundreds of books on real estate, self-improvement

reputation for closing deals and closing them on time, you get more deals. So honesty and integrity bring wealth to you.

Honesty is facing the facts and standing by them. This builds responsibility for your actions, which can ultimately lead to wealth.

For instance, you want to be honest with your contractors. Let them know when you are going to pay them and then pay them on time. Do not mask a problem that's going to develop in six months. Fix the problem the right way.

### Integrity

Integrity is promising the facts ahead of time and ultimately fulfilling that promise. It means doing what you say you're going to do within the time frame you say you're going to do it.

For example, if you tell someone you're going to close a deal within a certain time frame, do everything in your power to achieve this. I've seen investors put homeowners under contract just to hold the property and ultimately not close it, and the homeowners go through foreclosure. In my book, that's dishonest. And you've done nothing but create more problems in a person's life.

When you can't follow through on what you said, let people know as soon as possible. Explain why. Never be too proud to say "I'm sorry" or "I'm wrong." Ultimately, people will value you for having true integrity in your life.

Now, understand, there are varying circumstances. Things come up in life. But you want to do the absolute best to come

and leadership. Sometimes books are good, and sometimes they have gaps. I enjoyed the challenge of filling in the gaps and putting information together.

## Personal Economies

In 1986, when I was 16, I saw the real estate market and economy crash in Texas. People we knew from our community or my dad's company moved to Delaware, where the economy was good and they could find jobs. Meanwhile, in Texas, many people I knew started to have a gloomy outlook on money, the economy and life.

I realized that the economy could be good in one state, but bad in another. That opened my eyes up to what I call "rolling economies."

At 16, I also learned that an economy is not all-consuming. Even though Texas was going through a recession, some people were still making money. I saw that people who were not making money shut themselves down. They made less money, not because they were lazy, but because they believed that they could not make money.

When I was young, we participated in a community association where people seemed happy and positive. They were relaxed and at ease. People seemed to have more money. I loved going there because of their positive attitudes.

Later, we moved to a different community association — same organization, just different location. Some people were positive, but the majority seemed to have something negative happening in their lives. They were sick or sad. They often had some kind of a problem or they were trying to make ends meet or they talked about how money didn't grow on trees. They did not have enough money.

The change from a positive environment to a negative one had an

through on what you say you're going to do. This creates integrity and ultimately builds trust.

## More Money

You know what? By having honesty and integrity in your business, you actually create more money. Integrity and honesty are built from a mentality that there is more money out there. It actually reinforces the belief that there's enough for everyone to share.

Lying, deceit and dishonesty are based on fear. They come from the false belief that there's not enough money. Decisions made from fear are never the right decisions. A scarcity-based mentality will make you a very poor person, financially as well as emotionally.

Flipping houses is about creating wealth in your life, and wealth in your life involves great nights of sleep. That comes from knowing you have put in an honest day's work, which will ultimately lead to long-term money in your pocket.

When you are honest, you don't need to go to bed at night worrying about what you told somebody or if you have to cover it up the next day with a lie. This peace of mind contributes to a good lifestyle. However, just possessing honesty and integrity will not make you rich. These qualities will help you achieve wealth. You also need a strong motivation, your "why," and positive beliefs about money in order to get rich. Educating yourself will also provide rocket fuel to riches.

influence on me. I grew increasingly angry and frustrated when I was 16, 17 and 18 years old — not because I was misguided, but because we were around negative people.

I did not understand it at the time. But looking back, I realize there was a correlation between the negativity of the people we were spending time with and the amount of money they earned. At the time, I was not able to control who I was with on a daily basis. I believed that many of our friends and community members were going down. Many people were going down emotionally, as well as financially. It upset me.

It was easy to point our fingers at the economy, but, inherently, I knew deep inside it was the people with whom we were spending our time with that had the greatest effect on our own personal economy. We got caught up in their belief that money doesn't grow on trees.

By 18, I realized how important money truly is to people's overall happiness. A lot of people think that money does not buy you happiness. That may or may not be true, but money can certainly contribute to happiness. I knew a lot of people who were very broke, and they were not happy. I saw that people were never going to be happy if they cannot pay their bills, and they are totally stressed out financially.

But I held on to something deep inside me that said money is a good thing, money is positive. In my heart, I believed that I was running to save my financial soul.

In the movie "Twister," there's a scene where the actors are running for their lives, because there's this massive, dark tornado coming up behind them. They run inside a barn, and they hold onto two anchors like handlebars. Meanwhile, the tornado comes through, and everything around them gets blown away — the barn, the house, everything. Then they look up, and there's peacefulness and calm around them.

## Smart Work

I was raised to respect hard work. Now I believe in something even better: smart work.

Hard work will bring you a paycheck. Some of the hardest workers in the world are men who dig ditches. They get little to no respect and they have even less money. I love and I respect my parents for all the hard work they did. But my dad also said that if you can have money come to you, rather than having to chase a dollar, you can create big money in your life.

I have deals come to me all the time, so I don't have to chase the dollar. For me, it's not about hard work as much as about smart work.

I work smart by having systems in place that bring deals to me, so I'm not out knocking on doors all the time. I work smart by having systems that allow me to manage my contractors properly, so that projects get done within budget and on time. I work smart by using systems that bring buyers to the houses, instead of us chasing potential buyers. I work smart by allowing my money to generate more profits, rather than me pounding the pavement.

Hard work is good. Smart work is better.

## The Gift of Problems

The challenges that come up in life actually give us strength. I am a much stronger person today than when I started because of the challenges I have met, and I completely anticipate and

As a teenager, I felt like that. No matter how much turmoil, negativity and bad association was around me, and even though my youthful reaction was to be angry or frustrated, I held onto one single belief that has been the catalyst for my success, the belief that money is good. It kept me anchored, and it got me through those bad times.

Now that I have a lot of money, I realize how it can be positive. The lack of money tends to create stress, dissension and crime. There is talk about the bad things that happen when people have money, but they fail to acknowledge the bad things that happen when people do not have money.

**Family Rebel**

As I grew up, my dad switched jobs from being a teacher to selling aluminum siding and later starting a construction company. People might think that because my dad had a construction company, I learned the business. That is like saying if your dad was a doctor, you would know how to perform brain surgery by osmosis.

But the truth is I did not learn construction. I was very headstrong, and I did not want to labor in the Texas heat. I wanted to be a businessman. I completely stayed away from his business, except for the occasional trash pick-up assignments I was given. I was young, independent and I wasn't interested in being a construction worker; I wanted to be the boss.

Later, when I got into flipping houses, my dad was worried for me. "How can you flip houses with no construction experience?" he asked.

Well, it turns out that I did not need construction experience to run a successful business flipping houses. Even today, when people say they can't flip houses because they have no construction experience, I say they are simply grasping at straws.

look forward to becoming a much stronger person 10 years from now.

## Money as a Positive Force

Some people say that money cannot make you happy. But they do not talk about how the lack of money can make you unhappy.

Try being happy when you're fighting to keep your lights on. Try being happy when you cannot feed your family. Try being happy when you are buried in debt. Veronica and I experienced a tremendous amount of stress and were phenomenally unhappy when we were broke, she was recovering from surgery and we had no place to stay because our house had been foreclosed.

The highest crime rates are in the poorest neighborhoods because lack of money brings out something bad in people.

Money can create more happiness in life. It can generate more energy and a positive flow. Money is what gives people the ability to make things happen. Money is what drives charities.

By having additional money in your life, you can create more wealth, time, resources and education for your family. You can use money to help a sick loved one through his or her sickness. If you are planning for retirement, you can use money to plan for your future. You can also use money to make charitable donations and give back to your community.

Warren Buffet, the famed investor, is one of the greatest

My dad went to college, but he said it was not really necessary for me to go. Aside from math, he said, I would not need much of a college education in the real world unless I was going into the medical or legal field. And you know what? He's right. I never did go to college.

I spent a lot of my teenage years not knowing what I wanted to do. I once heard someone say, "Do what you love." Well, at age 16, I liked playing practical jokes but the "Candid Camera" gig was already taken.

However, I always knew I wanted to have my own business. I knew I wanted to make money, make a difference and be well-known for doing it. But I did not know what that would be.

examples of what money can do. He has committed to giving more than $30 billion to charity. Those charities bring so much goodness to the world.

By flipping houses, you can have a positive impact on the community and the U.S. economy. By flipping one house, you create income for suppliers – paint, roofing, wood, cabinets, closets. You generate work for contractors – carpenters, tilers, plumbers and landscapers, to name a few. All these people have families to support.

By selling a house, you help others involved in the sales process – real estate agents, mortgage brokers, lenders and processors. And when you sell a home, you are giving a family not just a place to live, but maybe even their dream home. You help fulfill their American dream.

Every time you fix and flip a house, it's like dropping a pebble in the water. The ripple effect creates money for so many other people and their families. The more houses you flip, the more lives you can affect in a positive way. By generating more money for yourself, you create more money for many others as well. By creating more wealth, you help lift the whole economy.

# Chapter 4

## How I Met Veronica
*Listening to My Dreams*

- **California Party**
- **Donut Shops**
- **Knock on the Door**
- **Together**

**California Party**

It was summer 1994, and I was 23 years old. I was in California hanging out with friends from San Antonio who had moved to Los Angeles.

My buddy Josh was getting married in less than a week. I stayed at my friend Steve's house, hanging out with him and his cousin, my good friend Aaron.

Little did I know that this was where I would meet the love of my life, my wife, the mother of my child, my most loyal fan, my muse, my inspiration, the best salesperson I would ever meet, my toughest negotiator and my closest business partner.

The weekend before the wedding, we went to a party in town. There were a lot of people and great music. I was so excited. I walked around the party thinking to myself, "Oh, man, this is fantastic!

# Chapter D

## Your Money Mentors
Business Masters Can Help Fuel Your Success

- **Mentors**
- **Environment of Empowerment**
- **Continuous Learning**
- **Your Inner Intelligence**

### Mentors

If you are going to grow, you want to walk in the footsteps of people who have done what you want to do. This helps reduce your learning curve and you will succeed faster.

Do not take financial advice from anyone who does not make at least twice as much money as you do. If you don't know friends or family who make more money than you, then you need to find somebody else to talk to about financial ideas or strategies. If you don't have someone, find a mentor. Find a coach. Find somebody who will support those dreams and teach you strategies for making money.

The average person has one million-dollar idea a year. You want to take that idea and hone, build and shape it until it comes to fruition.

This is Southern California!" Then I thought, "There must be some beautiful Southern California girls here!"

Soon, I started talking to a girl named Liz. After awhile, she said that I had to meet her cousin Veronica. Liz took me to Veronica and introduced us.

I thought Veronica was beautiful. She was tall, with long, dark-red curly hair and a great-looking tan. She seemed very sweet, innocent and young.

Veronica later said that when she first saw me, she thought to herself, "This is the kind of guy I need to stay away from. The other girls think he's cute, but he's not my type. This guy's full of himself, and he's nothing but trouble."

Veronica and I started chatting. My buddies started coming around, and we all talked to her. We all liked her.

Later, I danced with her a bit and I thought we were hitting it off well.

When it was time to leave, I asked Veronica for her phone number.

"Well, you can have my friend's phone number," she said.

"Thanks," I said, "but I asked for your phone number."

When she still refused, I explained that I was from Texas, and I wasn't in California very much.

She figured it was safe, so she gave me her number.

Not having a mentor – or not listening to one – can cost you a lot more money. I lost $60,000 on a deal because I was not willing to listen to my mentor, who told me to get more educated.

It was a humbling experience. The school of hard knocks is many times more expensive than learning from a master. In my case, my unwillingness to learn cost me $60,000.

### Environment of Empowerment

We've all heard that who you are is who you hang around with. But most people don't realize that your money is also who you hang around with.

If all you eat every day is beef jerky, eventually you're going to look like beef jerky. If all you put in your mind are old, dried-up negative thoughts, your brain will eventually be mental beef jerky.

But if you're putting healthy things into your body – vitamins, minerals, water, protein, complex carbohydrates – your body will look healthy. If you have friends and family who have positive mind-sets and make positive financial strides in their life, your mind will also be positive and be willing to accept more money.

Ultimately, your money is what your mind thinks. You cannot produce positive income with a negative mind-set. And you cannot have a positive financial mind-set while spending time with friends who have negative thoughts about money.

Understand, you can still love and care about your friends and family, but if they do not support your beliefs about money,

## Donut Shops

I called Veronica the very next day. We chatted awhile, and she said her parents owned a donut shop and that she lived in Chino Hills.

That afternoon, I looked up all the donut shops in Chino Hills and went to see her. I went to one place after another until I had gone to all 12 donut shops in Chino Hills. I realized that Southern California wasn't like San Antonio, where distances are not as long. By the time I left the last donut shop, it was about 9:30 p.m.

Finally, I called Veronica. Because I had only met her once, and I wasn't sure, I asked with all sincerity, "Is your family Asian?"

"No, why?" she said.

"Because I've been looking for you at all the donut shops in Chino Hills, asking for Veronica," I said. "All those stores had Asian shopkeepers."

She started laughing. "We live in Chino Hills, but the donut shop is in Santa Ana."

So I just proved my ignorance about things and the Southern California lifestyle.

"Well, I've been driving around Chino Hills looking for you. I wanted to see you," I said. "Can I go over to your house?"

Veronica said she had to ask her father. She called me back and said yes.

I went to Veronica's house with my buddy Aaron. By the time we got there, it was nearly 10:30 p.m. She invited us to the living room to watch a video, "Dumb and Dumber." It was very innocent.

then don't talk to them about money. You can talk about family things, sports, food and other things, but absolutely do not let them talk about money in your presence.

When you have negative friends around you, their level of income becomes acceptable for your life. It's a justification for where you are, because you want to fit in. When you are inspired to follow a lead on a house and make lots of money but your friends don't think it's a good idea, somewhere in your mind you will talk yourself out of going. And you think, "Well, I'm doing as well as they are."

People who have money have friends who support and help each other. As you grow in your investment career, you want to make friends with people who get excited for you when you find deals. You want friends who will be jazzed when you buy a great property.

Friends like this actually help you create more energy in your life. They give you the desire to do more deals, to make more money. They support you.

I remember what it was like when I was starting out and did not have friends around me who were incredibly successful in real estate. I felt a huge need for support in this area. I wanted an environment of empowerment.

Years later, when thousands of television fans asked me for advice on flipping houses, I remembered how important it was to create this environment of empowerment. I wanted my students to have a way to create positive peer pressure around them. I wanted to create shortcuts so my students would not have to work as hard or feel as lonely as I did during my early

A few minutes later, Veronica's dad came down.

"I didn't know you meant that they were coming over tonight," he said to Veronica. "This is not an appropriate time for him to be here. It's too late at night."

Aaron and I got up to leave. I could see Veronica turning red with embarrassment.

I said to Veronica's dad, "I respect that."

I shook hands with Veronica's dad and introduced myself. Then we left.

When we were in the car, Aaron said, "I can't believe you just left without a fight. You argue with everybody."

"You know what," I said, "That girl has a relationship with her father – a good relationship – and he's protective of her. That's the kind of girl I could marry. I respect him and his position. He's just protecting his daughter."

I knew I liked Veronica, and this made me want to get to know her more. I knew she was a good person, because she had been raised a certain way.

But I also just wanted to be friends with Veronica. I knew that if I dated her, I would want to marry her, and I wasn't ready to get married.

years. I created Web sites, blogs, workbooks, courses and a coaching team to give people the support they need to succeed.

I am constantly creating new strategies to make money. Along with my team of coaches, I teach my students money-making strategies. If you just need somebody to talk to, you may call one of my strategists to support you in your desire to make money.

I believe in creating that community because without a support system, you're taking something very simple and making it very difficult.

## Continuous Learning

Fans ask me this question again and again: "What if I have no money and no credit?" The answer is worth repeating again and again.

The No. 1 thing is to get an education, because that's how to learn to flip properties. A lot of people start flipping with no money, no credit and no education. The key to flipping with no money is to educate yourself.

There are only a few ways to create riches in your life:

1. Inheritance – Other people give you money, but you don't get a sense of satisfaction.

## Knock on the Door

A few months later, I took another trip to California. I was hooked on California – I loved Southern California – and I wanted to see Veronica.

I stayed at Steve's house again. I called Veronica and invited her to spend a day with us. She was attending a beauty college and would have to skip out early to join us. The next day, Steve and I picked her up at the beauty college, and we went to a park, hiked and had a good time.

When we drove her back, I asked Veronica if she would come and see me the next day, since I was flying back to San Antonio. She said she had school the next day, and she lived an hour's drive away from Steve's place in Whittier. She would not be able to see me.

Early the next morning, I had a dream about Veronica. In my dream, she was on her way to see me. Then, still dreaming, I saw her knock on the door. In my sleep, I knew that if she knocked on my door, it meant this was something long-term.

Suddenly, I awoke to a sound. I was in bed in Steve's house. It was about 8:30 in the morning. I heard knocking at the front door. This was real and live. I knew it was Veronica.

Steve went to get the door. It really was Veronica. He let her in, and she sat down on the living room sofa.

I got out of bed and went to the bathroom. I washed my face, brushed my teeth, gargled and fixed my hair. Then I walked out and sat down on the loveseat across from Veronica.

"Hi," she said, smiling softly. "I came to tell you goodbye."

2. Win the lottery – You win money. But most people who win the lottery lose it all within five years, according to the Money, Meaning and Choices Institute, which advises people who receive financial windfalls. I believe this is because most lottery winners lack education in managing money.

3. School of hard knocks – You learn from experience, but it is a very bumpy road with many detours and impasses.

4. Education – You learn from others through mentoring, seminars, books or CDs. This is ultimately what will bring you to a new financial level.

Wealthy people are constantly upgrading their knowledge and skills. They are constantly learning. Many millionaires I know read lots of self-help books. I recommend that if you want to become one, too, that you read at least 12 self-help books a year.

I read self-improvement and investment books during work weeks, and I read fiction when I go on vacation. Even though I never went to college, I have consistently advanced my education. I have read hundreds of books and listened to dozens of CDs on real estate investing.

All these books and CDs have helped improve my business. I also found a lot of gaps in the materials I read, such as where to find deals and how to run a flipping business like a regular business. By filling in these gaps and tinkering with various strategies, I have perfected a system that enables me to flip as many as 30 houses a month. When information is put together intelligently, I have found it to be very useful and profitable.

It's a lot of work becoming educated, and it seems insane to read dozens of books and listen to dozens of CDs. But it's not

## Together

Over the next three years, Veronica and I built a friendship over the phone. Once in a while, I'd fly out to Chino Hills, but we kept it very platonic.

I wanted to know that she and I could get along. I knew that when we really did start to date, this was something I wanted to last a long time. Veronica had a strong sense of commitment, and I knew I would be strongly committed to her, as well. But I was not ready to get married. It wasn't that I wanted to play the field. Emotionally, I just wasn't mature enough yet.

During that time, I worked all sorts of odd jobs selling men's suits, ladies' shoes, water filters and car oil.

My father said the only thing useful he learned in college was math. So I never went to college. I moved out of my parents' house at age 23 and lived in a rinky-dink, one-bedroom apartment.

In early 1997, Veronica and I finally started dating. I went from really liking her – and knowing that if I got really close, I would love her – to falling deeply in love with her.

We traveled back and forth between California and Texas. I didn't have much money, but I would spend my last dimes on cell phone bills to talk with her and on airplane tickets to see her, and vice versa.

At the end of the year, Veronica scraped up $400 for a plane ticket, packed up her things and flew to San Antonio to be with me. We got married in December 1997. I was 27 and she was 21.

as insane as the intense feeling of frustration that comes from being burdened with bills. It's not as insane as knowing that others are making tons of money, but you are not.

If you want to get wealthy, you need to know how to do it. Education and learning from others is the fastest way to do that. Reading this book is part of your education. Then actual experience flipping houses is the next step in your education.

You might read this book again one day and it will all seem much easier. You will have learned all that you are reading here. You will have conquered flipping houses and you will be looking for the next venture to take on. This book will have been one important step on your path to wealth.

## Your Inner Intelligence

If you're determined to create wealth for yourself and your loved ones, understand that if you think you can, you absolutely can.

You want to hold onto something inside yourself that knows you can succeed. I call that your inner intelligence. I define inner intelligence as the first thought you have before fear arises.

When I was growing up, I did not want to lose myself to other people's thought processes. Some people said I was rebellious, but I wanted to hold onto my beliefs that money could be good. So I closed my ears to negativity and listened to my inner intelligence.

# Chapter 5

## No Money, No Credit, Massive Debt
*How I Started with Nothing*

- **My Greatest Inspiration**
- **Blood Complications**
- **The Worst Day of My Life**
- **Medical Debt**
- **Food Stamps**
- **Foreclosure**
- **Living in a Garage**
- **The Turning Point**

### My Greatest Inspiration

Four months after our wedding, Veronica became pregnant. She started having medical complications immediately, and the doctors said it would be a difficult pregnancy.

Veronica wanted to be with her family during the pregnancy. I had just received a $4,500 settlement from a car accident, so we moved back to Southern California to be near her family.

The birth of my son was one of the happiest moments of my life. He became one of my greatest sources of inspiration and motivation. The first two years of his fragile life helped me realize my true reasons for wanting to succeed in life. If not for him and Veronica, I

As you go into real estate, some people might tell you that you cannot do it, the market isn't right, you should get a job or you're crazy. But your inner intelligence must say that you can. Maybe you picked up this book because your inner intelligence said there's something here for you. Maybe your inner intelligence said there's something beyond other people's limiting beliefs. Trust your inner intelligence.

Whatever challenges you run into, your inner intelligence will know what to do. Whenever you face difficulties, go back to your inner intelligence. It is always correct.

would not have pushed as hard as I did to excel in business. The trials and tribulations we went through during these years also taught me to be honest with myself and to have compassion for others facing dire challenges.

My son was born in January 1999. We named him after my father and myself: Armando. But Veronica nicknamed him "Mondo Man," and it stuck.

## Blood Complications

Mondo Man was born with a lot of medical complications. He looked great, but his body was fighting a battle inside. He had a rare blood disease that put his life at risk.

The problem resulted because Veronica and I have incompatible blood types. Our baby got a bad combination of both: He inherited my type A blood, and Veronica's O type antigens, which destroys type A red blood cells. Our baby suffered anemia and possible internal bleeding. Because his platelet count was so low, his blood could not clot and he could bleed to death with very little provocation.

Because of his condition, our baby had to be taken to Children's Hospital in Los Angeles, an hour's drive away.

While that was going on, another complication arose. We were in Los Angeles visiting my son at the hospital. Suddenly, I heard a sound that I will never forget. It was the most desperate scream I have ever heard. Veronica ran through the waiting room and into the men's restroom. I ran after her.

When I found her, it looked like a crime scene. I saw blood splattered on the walls, floors and all over Veronica. She had lost

# Chapter E

## Your Money Mind
Success Begins with Your Thoughts

- **Limitations**
- **Myths and Facts**
- **Analysis Paralysis**
- **Critical Moment**
- **Know Your "Why"**
- **Assets List**
- **Daily Actions**
- **Make Mistakes**

### Limitations

You might say that you can't invest in real estate because you have no money, no credit or no business experience.

I did not have any of those either. But if I can make money investing in real estate, so can you. The only thing that holds us back is our thoughts.

Having any one of these limitations is no longer an excuse not to succeed. It is only a limitation you set for yourself.

nearly half of the blood in her body, which we later learned was due to complications from her Caesarian operation.

After the doctors stabilized her, she was transported by ambulance to where she had given birth in Upland. They had to keep her in the emergency ward.

## The Worst Day of My Life

For weeks, I drove back and forth between my son's and my wife's hospitals, an hour away from each other. After several weeks, Mondo Man was discharged. Veronica was still in the hospital. Now I had to take Mondo Man for frequent checkups.

During one of the checkups, the doctors found that Mondo Man had taken a turn for the worse. His platelet count had dropped dramatically.

I checked him into the emergency room, and I was a nervous wreck again. Mondo Man stayed in the hospital for several days, while I had many sleepless nights. After many days of driving between the hospitals to see Mondo Man and Veronica, the doctors finally released Veronica to go home.

Veronica was nervous about being alone at home, so I called Mondo Man's nurse and told her I would not be there that night, because I needed to be with Veronica. I asked the nurse to take extra special care of Mondo Man tonight. She gladly agreed.

Veronica and I woke up the next morning in horror. She was lying in a pool of her own blood. During the night, she had lost nearly half of the remaining blood in her body.

## Myths and Facts

To make money, you must have the right money mind-set. Here are the common myths about flipping houses – and the facts.

**Myth:** I can't buy houses with bad credit.
**Fact:** Lenders lend to people who flip houses. They look at the deal, not the borrower.

**Myth:** There are no good deals in my area.
**Fact:** There has never been a better time to find great deals than now. There are always great deals if you know where to look.

**Myth:** I have no business experience.
**Fact:** Most people who run successful businesses started with no business experience. You can overcome the lack of experience with education.

**Myth:** I have failed so often, I feel destined to fail.
**Fact:** Because you failed so many times, you're one step closer to success.

I rushed her to the emergency room. The doctors said her condition was severe and that they would have to perform an emergency hysterectomy.

I remember being fully conscious, but it felt like I was almost not there. The noise from the heart monitor machine sounded like a car alarm going off in my head.

Doctors scrambled to prep for the emergency surgery. Nurses looked at me with a great sense of impending doom.

I heard the sobering words from the head surgeon: "Armando, say goodbye to your wife. This may be the last time you will ever speak to her."

Just after the head surgeon told me the news, he left the room to let me have a few minutes with my wife. Veronica's face was pale and turning blue. But she could still speak.

I told Veronica about the doctor's prognosis. Then I said, "That's bullshit. That's the most ridiculous thing I ever heard."

I looked Veronica straight in her eyes and said: "You start telling yourself you are healthy and you are strong."

She rolled her eyes.

I held her and said, "I want you to say it, too. 'I am healthy. I am strong.'"

"You're crazy," she said.

"I am healthy and I am strong," I said.

"I am healthy. I am strong," said Veronica.

**Myth:** I have no construction experience.

  **Fact:** Construction is not rocket science. What you need is a good subcontractor agreement, budget sheets and a way to control your projects. Once you educate yourself on how to budget for a property and have subcontractor agreements in place, you know 80 percent of how to run the construction part of a flip.

**Myth:** I have no time.

  **Fact:** With a proven system, you do not have to spend all your time flipping houses. The system works for you so that you don't have to spend all your time doing it.

I told her to say it, over and over again, "I am healthy. I am strong."

"I am healthy. I am strong." She said it so many times, she started to laugh.

When the doctor came back and heard her words, he said, "I am going to do the best I can do as a doctor. Whether you live or not is up to you."

After Veronica came out of surgery I sat next to her while she slept. That is when I got a call to rush down to the hospital where Mondo Man was located.

Once I arrived there, his doctor told me, "I have never seen a child in such bad condition live. He may not make it past the next 48 hours."

On the same day, I was told by each of their respective doctors that my son and wife might not live past the next 48 hours. That was the toughest day of my life.

## Medical Debt

Several months later, Veronica and Mondo Man were released from their hospitals. I felt fortunate and blessed that they both survived. But they still had a long road to recovery. Veronica was 22, and she grieved that she would never be able to have children again.

I spent the next year taking care of them and nursing them back to health. I attended to Veronica, fed our baby, changed his diapers, bought groceries, gave them their medicine, took them to the doctors and paid the bills.

I could no longer work. I had to stay home and take care of them.

The more you focus on the facts, the more power you will have flipping houses. The more you have the right money mind-set, the more you will attract money in your life.

## Analysis Paralysis

If you raise your standards for what you believe you deserve, you will raise the standards for your lifestyle. Never be paralyzed by your thoughts. Go with your inner intelligence – it will move you to take action.

If you have analysis paralysis, you will not only freeze your dreams, but ultimately, your entrepreneurial spirit and freedom. Analysis paralysis creates a prison for financial and emotional freedom.

## Critical Moment

You may have felt at some point in your life that the time for change is now. That is a critical moment. That is the time to take action.

When you fall upon hard times, it is the time to realize your true inner resources. You cannot use hard times as an excuse for long.

As you're reading this, you may be having your own critical moment. Maybe you were fired from your job. Maybe you lost your house. Maybe you are facing family challenges. Understand that when these things happen, there is a reason and an opportunity. If you do not take advantage of the opportunity, the reason can become an excuse.

I tried selling cars for a while, but frankly, I was just not cut out be a car salesman. My biggest challenge was that my mind was distracted by my wife and son's fragile conditions. I didn't produce much income, which meant I wasn't paying my bills. Soon, the bill collectors came knocking on the door.

I had $50,000 in medical and miscellaneous debt. I knew that I would never be able to pay off that debt working at a regular job making $40,000 to $50,000 a year, but I wasn't able to even make that. Since moving to California, I had worked or thought about working as a pizza delivery driver, painter, car salesman and entrepreneur. But all that had led to nothing.

## Food Stamps

Nothing is more humiliating for a man than not being able to provide for his family. It was different than, but equally as hard as, being told in the same day that my wife and son were going to die.

I remember the day I went to fill out a food stamp application. The welfare office had vinyl floors. It was crowded with people waiting in long lines and babies crying. I never thought I would end up needing food stamps. I thought about what my family and friends would think if they knew I was living on food stamps. It was gut-wrenching. I felt so ashamed.

But it also was cleansing. It forced me to face the truth that I had no money.

The worst thing was actually using those food stamps. I did not want to use those stamps, but I had to buy food. Once, I went to the supermarket, and I put seven to eight items at the checkout counter. The woman at the register was probably in her 40s. She asked if I would like to pay by cash, check or credit card. I handed her the food stamps.

Once the reason becomes an excuse, you are no longer taking responsibility for your actions. Once you stop taking responsibility for your actions, you lose control of your life. And ultimately, you lose your freedom.

A critical moment is when your inner intelligence signals it is time to make a change in your life. That's the time to take action.

You can:

- Call a mentor
- Scan the Internet for deals
- Look for a real estate agent
- Call us at 1-800-771-6202 x 4001

By taking action now, you can pursue your golden opportunity to create your own fortune. In just a few years, you could be telling your own amazing life story. You could be sharing your story with your children, significant other or friends. You could be writing your own life book.

**Know Your "Why"**

It is important to know why you are doing this business. Once you know your "why," you will be motivated to keep working through the hard times, to overcome obstacles that you hit.

You have to have a strong enough "why" to keep going.

She looked at the food stamps, and then she looked at me, then back at the stamps. It seemed she was trying not to be judgmental, but she couldn't hide it. I could hear her wondering why a healthy and capable-looking man like me was using food stamps. I could not bear the weight of my shame. I hung my head low.

It was very painful. But I also thought that I was now paying for not preparing earlier in life to make money. It was the reward I reaped for all those small decisions not to apply myself.

For the next two years, I was on and off food stamps and unemployment insurance. That experience forced me to look at myself and take responsibility. I had to admit that when I had met Veronica, I could have been learning something, but I wasn't. When I started working, I could have educated myself, but I did not. I asked myself, "Did I watch too much TV? Yes. Did I drink too much beer? Yes." All those small decisions had led to this result.

It was not just the hospital operations that had gotten me here. It was the unconscious decision to not educate myself. Instead, I had occupied my time with frivolous activities, which left me unprepared for the challenges of life.

## Foreclosure

When we moved back to Southern California, my father-in-law lent me $4,000 to buy a little condominium. It was in Ontario, where Veronica had grown up and just 30 minutes from her parents' house. This is where we now lived.

After the operations, I did not earn enough to pay the mortgage. I missed one payment, then two and three. At the time, I did not know anything about real estate investors who help homeowners get out of foreclosure situations. I did not think there was anything I could do.

Here's how to know your "why." Ask yourself:

- Who am I doing this for?
- Who or what is the greatest inspiration in my life?
- What is the legacy I want to leave?

Think ahead to the day you are going to die. Ask yourself:

- Will I be disappointed with myself?
- Will I have accomplished everything I wanted to do?
- Will I have lived up to my potential?
- What will I have left for others?

The answers to these questions will give you your "why" for flipping houses. The larger your answers can be, the stronger your motivation will be to succeed.

**Assets List**

Instead of focusing on what you do not have, make a list of your assets. The right type of assets list will open your creative mind.

Here are some questions you can ask to create your list:

- Which country do I live in?
- Do I have the freedom to open a business?
- Do I have a brain?
- Do I have at least average intelligence?
- Can I read?

The lender foreclosed on our condominium, and I lost the $4,000 that my father-in-law loaned me. It was very painful. It was very difficult to tell him, "Abel, I just got foreclosed on, and I don't have the money to pay you back."

My father-in-law is one of the most gracious people I've ever met, and he told me it was no big deal. He was more concerned about me taking care of my family.

## Living in a Garage

We moved into my in-laws' garage. This was not a converted garage. It was a two-door garage with a divider down the middle. We pushed the lawn mower and weed eater to one side and moved into the other side.

We threw down a rug and put in our bed and TV. Our clothes hung on an exposed closet rod. We had our shoes and boxes of stuff on the ground. Everything else was piled into the other side of the garage.

At night, the three of us shared the double bed. It was June 2001, and the garage had no air-conditioning, so it was very hot.

Veronica's parents gave us food and clothes for our baby. My in-laws are gracious and generous people, and they never held it over my head. But I was determined to one day prove that I could provide for their daughter and grandson.

## The Turning Point

One day, Veronica and Mondo Man were relaxing on the bed in the garage. As I walked in from the utility room around the corner, I saw them watching the video "101 Dalmatians."

- Can I find information on the Internet?
- Can I call people on the phone?
- Can I find people to coach me?
- Is there real estate where I live?
- Do people need houses where I live?

Of course, these are just simple things. But keep adding up your assets. Soon you will see that your assets outweigh your liabilities. You have more than you think you do.

Here's what else you can do:

- Put your assets list up on the wall.
- Add to the list every week.
- Focus on your assets, not your liabilities.

As you do your real estate flipping, keep thinking about your assets. You have what you need to be successful.


**Daily Actions**

You cannot make money without taking action. All the small decisions add up to your larger results.

In times of economic recession, a small number of people take action and make 50 times more money than people who just twiddle their thumbs. That is how the economy really works. Most people think the economy is dictated by inflation, the government, housing, the stock market or this or that. But the economy is dictated by people.

I looked at them and thought to myself, "This is not so bad. This is OK." I was satisfied. I was content.

As I headed back to the utility room, it hit me. I thought, "What the hell did I just do? My standards have fallen so low that this way of life is acceptable to me? It's OK for my family to live in a garage, to live on food stamps and not be living the life they deserve?"

I realized that with the hard times, I somehow lost a part of myself. I had let my standards fall so low that I almost thought it was OK to live in a garage and on food stamps.

I decided that I could no longer use hard times as an excuse. I had to make an immediate change. I knew that real change would come only if I made a choice at that moment to change my life — even if it was scary.

I knew I had to do it before I tried to "think it through," before I got "analysis paralysis." I was scared. But my inner intelligence told me that now was the time to decide to be successful and achieve my dreams.

I knew I wanted to move back to Texas, where I could start over. California was filled with too many tough memories for me by now. I was the guy who made all these bad decisions and failed miserably. I wanted a fresh start.

I grabbed the cordless phone on the bed, and stepped out of the garage. I paced the sidewalk outside as I called my father.

"Hi, Dad," I said, "I need you to do me a favor. I need to borrow $1,000."

After explaining our living conditions, I said: "I'm not living up to my capabilities. I want to go back to Texas to raise my family. I need to make a radical change."

Your personal economy is dictated by your daily actions.

If somebody smokes every day, one day he or she will develop emphysema and lung cancer. That person might say, "Oh, my gosh! I'm sick. Why did this have to happen to me?" But it was the small actions they took every day that built up the problem.

Or if you run every day, you become very fit. My father is 73 years old and runs six miles a day. His family has a history of heart disease. But he cut fast food from his diet a long time ago, and he began running. It's the small, everyday actions that keep him physically strong and makes him look like a man in his early 60s.

So it is with growing wealthy. It's the small actions that we take every day – especially during challenging times – that ultimately create the outcome of whether we are rich or poor.

I know people who go home at 4:30 p.m. every day and watch television. They pop some beers and watch TV for hours. Other people tool around in their cars, mow the grass, and do things that make them feel busy but do not get them anywhere. They do not work on generating income and they never move up.

If you do something every day to invest in real estate, you can achieve your financial goals. When you get off work, go look at properties. Work on your flipping business. You can start generating profits.

Those small daily actions will add up. In two to 10 years, you can build a large saving for your retirement account and build financial security. Or you can greatly improve your lifestyle and the quality of your life. There is no single big action that

"I'll see what I can do," Dad said.

We hung up, and I got ready to move. Even if I could not borrow the money, I knew I would find a way to get back.

But Veronica did not want to go. "I'm not moving to Texas!" she said.

In California, she at least had a roof over her head and food to eat. Veronica's No. 1 priority was creating a home for our newborn son, and I had no job or money in Texas.

I told Veronica that I had to go with my instinct, that this was a critical moment that could change our lives forever. I told her we needed to raise our standards. She finally agreed to go.

A couple of days later, my dad called and said he could lend me $1,000. One week later, I rented a big Ryder truck, we packed up, and we headed for Texas.

is going to make a huge difference. It's the series of small ones – done consistently every day – that add up to big changes in your life.

## Make Mistakes

Be willing to make mistakes. The faster you make mistakes, the sooner you will reach your goal.

1. Set your ego aside. Your ego doesn't want you to make mistakes and ultimately prevents you from getting started.

2. Know that you will make mistakes.

3. Relish your mistakes. This points the finger back at me. I was broke and on food stamps when I rode into town on my last tank of gas. I hung my head very low. But my prior failures have now become my calling card for success. People used to call me flaky; now they call me ambitious. Relish the mistakes that you make.

4. Learn from your mistakes. Do not repeat them.

5. Learn how to create opportunity.

6. Learn how to create opportunity without mistakes. This will be discussed in a later chapter.

Obviously, the goal is to minimize mistakes. The point here is to understand that perfection does not exist, so do not expect it. Perfectionism can be an excuse for not getting started. Use mistakes as a learning tool, but use them wisely.

# Chapter 6

## Return to San Antonio
### *My Promise to Veronica*

- The Long Drive
- Promise to Veronica
- Last Tank of Gas
- The Biggest Regret
- A Husband's Motivation
- Bad Economy
- Creating My Assets List
- Assuming Success

### The Long Drive

The drive from Chino Hills to San Antonio takes three days with a family. It's a drive that crosses cities, towns, deserts, highways, dusty roads and lots of open spaces.

That gave me a lot of time to think. I wondered, "What am I going to do in Texas? How will I support my family?"

I needed cash immediately. I could not afford to wait around for something. I thought about starting a salsa company, making a business out of Veronica's delicious sauces. But I would need money to start a factory. It would be a one- to two-year ramp-up period, and I did not know anything about the food-processing business.

One shortcut is to learn from others' mistakes. That's why you need to get an education. When you learn from others, you minimize your mistakes. Find mentors who will show you the ropes, so you can reduce your learning curve.

I needed something that could generate cash immediately. It had to be something I could easily understand. It had to be tangible. And it had to be something I knew would work.

As the thoughts ran through my head, I remembered reading once that a vast majority of millionaires created their wealth through real estate. It is a real business, not some scam. Real estate is all around us. And everyone needs a home. Maybe this was something I could do.

Then I thought about doing rental properties. That might make $100 to $300 a month on cash flow, but not be enough for us to live on. And I did not have the credit to buy houses. Next, I considered flipping houses. I knew people could make a lot of money in it. It was real. It was something I could understand and was interested in. And if I could turn houses around quickly, I could make some cash.

I decided to flip houses once I got to San Antonio. I would have to hit the ground running, but that's what I would do. I did not have any money or credit. I really did not have anything on my side. But I was desperate. And my fear was gone, because the fear of being out on the streets was bigger than the fear of failing in business.

**Promise to Veronica**

We stopped at a little roach motel in Arizona during the trip. The next morning, we woke up to a beautiful sunrise. The sky was an amazing blue-gray. The desert around us was stark and beautiful. But we needed to hit the road. I felt a great sense of urgency inside. I felt the pressure of being broke.

As we left the motel, Veronica, our son and I started walking toward the Ryder truck. Suddenly, Veronica stopped. "You've taken me away from my family. You've taken me away from my security and everything I know," she said. "I'm your wife, and I'll go with you.

# Chapter F

## Make Money in Any Market
Deals Dictate Success, Whether the Market is Up, Down or Flat

- **Flip in Any Market**
- **Buy a Property, Not a Market**
- **Falling Markets**
- **Flat Markets**
- **Rising Markets**
- **Rolling Strategies**

### Flip in Any Market

After building my business base in San Antonio, I plan to flip houses across the country. My system works all across the nation – in different markets, with different houses. I'm not relegated to just one market or one state. Others elsewhere also have the opportunity to tap into my system.

Regardless of where I flip, the basic principles are the same: find motivated sellers, solve other people's problems, buy at a discount, control costs and use different selling strategies.

But there's more to life than just making money."

"What the hell are you talking about?" I said. "I'm desperate. I gotta make some money!"

She kept calm. Then she said: "I want you to make me a promise."

I kept my mouth shut – for once.

She continued: "If you learn the secrets of success, I want you to promise you will share them with the world. Success is not to be hoarded, it is to be shared."

"I promise," I said.

I took my promise seriously. I did not make it just to get her out of the way or shut her up. I could see that she was very sincere about it, and I knew she was right.

As we drove down that highway, I knew I needed to create a business that I could one day share with others. I wanted something that I could understand and would be easily understood by others. Ultimately, no matter what my situation was, I liked helping people. That promise motivated me. If I ever learned the secrets of success, I decided I would one day share it with the world.

### Last Tank of Gas

I had budgeted $1,000 to move. It cost $1,032 to move from Chino Hills to San Antonio. We rode into town on my last tank of gas.

Fortunately, just outside San Antonio is hilly country. As I was running out of gas, I managed to hit the downhills and glided into town, where we pulled in front of an apartment complex offering

## Buy a Property, Not a Market

I don't buy anything at full price. Whether it's a car or house, there are always people offering a discount and a deal.

Let's say you find a house that in a good market is worth $600,000, but in a slow economy is worth $450,000 and you can pick it up for $280,000. Does the market dictate what you do or does the property dictate what you do?

Properties and the deal dictate how you do business. It is not the market that dictates it. Markets do not dictate my power to buy a property. The property dictates whether to buy.

## Falling Markets

In a falling market, the house will not be worth the current market price after six months. Your best insurance is to buy it extremely under value, so even if you lose some equity, at least you will not be upside down on the property.

The slower the market, the more undervalued you want to buy properties. You want to buy houses that are 50 cents, 40 cents or even 30 cents on the dollar. That's an insurance policy against paying thousands to hundreds of thousands of dollars out of your pocket.

Let's say you live in San Francisco. Maybe your house is worth $800,000 now. But as prices decrease, your house might be worth $650,000 in a year. What I suggest you do is look for a deal for $450,000. Buy that house and sell the one you are living in.

three weeks' free rent to new tenants.

When I met the manager, I negotiated two and a half months' free rent for a two-bedroom apartment at $800 a month. I figured that in two and a half months, I could at least make money for rent.

That's how I learned that everything is negotiable. Years later, people often asked me, "Why are you such a stickler for budgets? Why do you negotiate so hard?" Well, originally, I did it out of survival. Once you have negotiated for survival, you can negotiate anything.

The next day, Veronica started selling our furniture for food money. She sold our dressers and a TV cabinet and made $430. That was enough for food and gas. It also was enough for me to buy business cards and a cell-phone plan with a free phone.

Veronica and I were committed to making it work. She shopped frugally. We ate at home. We ate sandwiches for lunch. I knew that if the electricity bills did not get paid, I could fight the utility company for a month and a half before they turned off the lights.

We had arrived in early August 2001. But by September, I was still looking for my first real estate deal, and I was under pressure to make rent by mid-October.

## The Biggest Regret

Then the terrorist attacks of Sept. 11, 2001 struck. On that fateful day, I got a phone call from a relative telling me to turn on my television. I sat in the living room, glued to the TV, along with the rest of America. I stared at the TV for 12 consecutive hours, watching news report after news report.

I thought about all of those lives that had suddenly ended. I

I know some of you are reading this book and saying, "You can't find those kinds of deals!"

Oh yeah? They're easier to find than in hot marketplaces.

I would pick up a deal in the $400,000 range. Then I would do a short sale through a bank because those sellers get very, very motivated.

Your $800,000 house already has equity in it. I suggest putting it on the market for about $680,000, or 15 percent to 20 percent under market value so you can move it and pull out that equity.

I suggest buying a property that's greatly undervalued because it would be like having an insurance policy. Because of that insurance you do not have to lose tens, and possibly hundreds of thousands, of dollars in equity. Make that move quickly, before everyone else wises up and does the same.

Maybe your property will sit on the marketplace for a while. But if your property value has gone up 100 percent say, over the last four years, taking a 20 to 25 percent discount now still leaves you with a 75 percent gain. Then find another property that is valued at 40 to 50 cents on the dollar. You have now insured yourself against losing tens to hundreds of thousands of dollars.

Perhaps you have a house valued at the current median price of $800,000. Feeling the pulse of the market, you believe that in two years the market is going to go down 20 percent. That would make your house worth $640,000.

wondered what kind of plans those individuals had made for their lives. What had they dreamed about? What had they missed when their lives were cut short?

I wondered, if I had died that day, what would be the hardest part? Leaving my family without a husband and father would be horrible.

Then the scariest thought in the world hit me. The worst thought would be if during my time on Earth, I had not lived up to my potential. I would be disappointed in myself for not doing my very best.

I was terrified by the thought of not becoming the person I was capable of being. Then, I thought, what if my son realized that his dad had not lived up to his potential? I realized that living up to my capabilities and being an example for my son was the greatest reason in life that I had to be successful.

I did not want my son to grow up thinking I was a loser. He thought I was big and strong now, but that would change as he grew older. I wanted him to be proud of me, to know that his dad was a success.

That became my overwhelming "why" for what I do. That became my motivation to succeed. Later, when I hit challenges and obstacles in my business, this is what pushed me to succeed.

## A Husband's Motivation

I also wanted to keep my promises to my wife. When we were dating, I had promised to provide for her and our family and give us a good life. So far, I had not fulfilled them.

That's what happens with many men. Early in the relationship, we're like peacocks. We show our feathers and make a tremendous amount of vows. Then one day we get married and forget our promises.

I suggest looking for a motivated seller with the same type of house. I would look for an $800,000 house, selling for 40 to 50 cents on the dollar. That means you want to pick up a house for around $450,000.

You might think that's impossible. But I guarantee I could fly out to San Francisco right now and find that deal within a month. With the rising number of foreclosures, the market is becoming flooded with motivated sellers and banks are going to become even more motivated to sell. If you know how to structure short sales and buy the right way, you will be able to find those deals.

So you will have created an insurance policy for yourself at 50 cents on the dollar. But, let's say in two years your property drops in value to $650,000. You will still have $150,000 equity in the property.

Let's say over the last four years, your property may have gone up 100 percent. So, originally, it was $400,000. Let's say it's now worth $800,000. You put $400,000 in your pocket. Let's say you sell that property today at 20 percent under market value. That means you'll be selling that property at a very attractive price of $640,000. That means you put $240,000 in your pocket.

So you buy a new property for $450,000, but it's worth $800,000. When the value drops to $650,000, you still have $200,000 equity in your house, plus the other $240,000 that you've made. You just bought yourself an insurance policy and doubled your equity and cut your losses.

What women want is very simple. They want our loyalty and commitment, and they want us to fulfill our promises.

Up to that time, I had not kept my promises to my wife by not providing financially for us. Veronica stuck with me, because she is a very loyal person. But if I put our family out on the street, she would have the right to leave me and I could not blame her. That became another huge motivation for me. I wanted to keep my promises to my wife.

## Bad Economy

After 9/11, people were in shock and grief. The economy froze throughout the country, and the housing market in Texas came to a standstill.

The real estate economy in San Antonio was already depressed. Many of the houses were infected with mold, which scared buyers. Houses sitting on the market were discounted as much as 50 percent.

Many people thought that they could not make money in a bad real estate market. I was just getting started then, but if I knew then what I know now, I could have retired after my first two years in business. Over the years, I came to see that people can make money in real estate whether the market is bad, flat or good. It is possible to make money in any market.

## Creating My Assets List

Of course, at the time, I had not landed a single deal yet. I did not know how. I just knew that I wanted to succeed for my son and wife.

I also knew that I had to stop feeling sorry for myself. I had to stop

## Flat Markets

In a flat market, you can do the same as in a cold market.

If it's a flat market that has not reached its peak, it has the potential to become a hot market. In that case, do not buy a house for more than 70 percent of market value. At 70 percent, you are relatively safe, because the market typically becomes hot in the next two or three years, so you will still make money.

If the market is flat because it already reached its peak, then I would do the same thing that I did in the cold market – which is to buy it at 30 to 50 cents on the dollar. That gives you insurance as the market begins to fall.

## Rising Markets

In a hot market, it's very simple. You buy at a maximum of 70 percent of the market value, including closing costs and repairs.

So you want to buy an $800,000 house at 70 percent, which is $560,000. In a fast market, that property will sell quickly, giving you a profit of $240,000, minus any holding costs and real estate agent fees.

## Rolling Strategies

Economies do not dictate my money. Economies simply dictate the strategy that I use to make money. When Texas was going through economic recession in the 1980s, I noticed that many people still made money. A national house-flipping franchise even set up shop in Texas during that time period.

focusing on what I did not have. Then, one day, my thinking shifted. I asked myself, "What do I have? What are the things I have going for me that will help build my flipping business?"

I began adding things to my assets list that would help me be successful in business.

I had a dialogue with myself:

"Where do I live?"

"America. The land of the free."

"Yep, that's an asset."

"I have the freedom to open a business and go and come as I please. That's another asset."

"I have a brain. Necessary asset."

"I have at least average intelligence. Another useful asset."

"I have the desire to be successful."

"I have access to free information via the Internet."

"I can read."

Though my list may sound generic to most, I knew that it would at least give me a mindset that I had valuable and tangible assets on my side. I placed my focus on all the things that could help me. I realized that my assets list far outweighed my liabilities list. I stacked the assets list high and deep.

During the recession, many wise people bought up properties. They made a tremendous amount of money by holding these properties while the rents were very high. When they sold their properties a few years later, when the market recovered, they made millions of dollars.

Do not let economies dictate your money. Let strategy dictate your money. Let the market determine which strategy to use, but let the strategy determine how much money you make.

During the Texas recession, people also moved to states with better economies. Now, with cell phones, the Internet and a global economy, you can easily do business in other markets without having to actually move. You can flip in your own backyard, in other states or even other countries. You can use technology to roll with economies around the world.

In hard times, many people throw their hands up and say, "Well, it's an economic recession." Then they go home at 5 p.m., turn on the television and complain that it's just too tough to make money right now. And they leave their financial destiny to the "gods of money."

By having a system and an education, you will be able to do something that most people do not do: make money flipping houses in any market and any location.

My liabilities list only read like this:

"No money. No credit. No experience."

After that, I always reminded myself that my assets far outweighed those liabilities. Every week, I would build on my assets list. It gave me the mental fuel to keep going.

## Assuming Success

After that, my thinking shifted again. I just assumed I was going to be successful. I gave my brain no other choice.

I had already spent 30 years wondering if I was going to be successful, thinking that one day I would be successful. The change I made in my mind was that now I was going to make it happen.

Once I assumed and lived like I was successful, I became a magnet. I started to attract success. Things started to happen.

# Chapter G

## How to Find Deals
Solving Homeowners' Problems First

- **Deals Before Money**
- **Find Motivated Sellers**
- **How to Negotiate with Homeowners**
- **WIIFM Radio**

### Deals Before Money

One of the questions that fans most often ask me is, "Where do I find the money?"

That is the most wrong, backward question to ask. I will tell you later where to find money. But this is the principle to remember: deals come before money.

Remember this: First you find the deal, then you find the money, then you find the contractor, then you flip the house.

The key is to find the deal first. Money always follows the deal.

When I started flipping houses, I didn't know that either. I was lost in the same lies as everybody else. I was freaked out and worried. "Where am I going to get the money? I don't have

# Chapter 7

## My First Deal
*Taking Action*

- **Chasing Fire Trucks**
- **Insurance Agent's Call**
- **Lisa's Story**
- **Finding the Money**
- **Selling the Property**

### Chasing Fire Trucks

I had two and a half months to make rent, and I needed to start finding houses immediately.

After all those medical bills, collection after collection and a real estate foreclosure, my credit score was dismally low at 501. This meant that I did not qualify for a traditional mortgage. I could not rely on conventional ways of investing in real estate.

One day, I was browsing in a bookstore. I breezed through some real estate books. I didn't really understand what they were talking about, but they said something about "motivated sellers." I thought, "OK, that's something to hang my hat on."

What that meant was you can't make money on a $200,000 house by buying it for $200,000. You need to buy houses from motivated sellers whose houses are undervalued.

money! I don't have credit!" I had no money and a 501 credit score – which does not qualify me for any kind of loan. I didn't know the answer then. But now I do.

Before I found a deal, I went to banks looking to see who would loan me money even though I had awful credit. I was committed to my dream of real estate riches, but the banks turned me down.

Once I found my first deal, I was able to find people who were willing to lend me the money because I gave them a great return on their investment. I learned to find the deal first, because the money will always follow.

You see, everyone wants a higher rate of return on their money. Even if you have bad credit scores, the right kind of lenders will do deals with you. They will even give you extra money to repair the house.

Why are they so willing? The reason is simple. They make more money and the loan is secure against real estate. They give you money based just on the deal itself. They do not need to look at your credit. They look at the deal.

The right lenders see no difference between me and anyone reading this book. It doesn't matter if you're a professional flipper with a TV show or if you're a beginner. They lend money based on the deal.

Your first thought should always be to find the deal. Create the discipline in your thinking. Once you find the deal, you can take it to people who have money. Without the deal, nobody will consider lending to you because they would be lending

I thought, "I've got to find motivated sellers." However, the book didn't say how to find them. I began to think about where these motivated sellers might be hiding. Then, I thought, "Well, who's more motivated than people whose houses are burning down?"

So I started chasing fire trucks. That's how little I knew. But it made sense to me. It was August 2001 in Texas, where the air is dry and temperatures can reach more than 100 degrees. Fires happened frequently.

I would be out driving, and as soon as I heard a fire truck siren, I would make a U-turn and follow it. Or Veronica would watch the 5 p.m. news and call me about a house that was burning down. They would usually announce the address on the news, so I would go there.

I'd show up at people's houses while their houses were still burning down. Everything would be crispy and smell like smoke. The firefighters might still be putting out the flames.

Then I would walk up to the homeowner and hand out my business card. "Sir" or "Ma'am," I said. "If you need me to buy your house, I'd be happy to help." A lot of homeowners flicked their middle fingers at me.

I did that for three to four weeks. I probably chased about 20 fire trucks. But it wasn't working. I decided that was not a good time to be handing out my business cards.

## Insurance Agent's Call

Then I got a phone call from an insurance agent.

"Hi, may I speak to Mr. Montelongo?" she said.

based on air. However, people will lend based on real estate all the time.

## Find Motivated Sellers

How do you find great deals? Find motivated sellers. These are homeowners facing challenges and selling their house helps solve that challenge.

Four main things create motivated sellers. It's what I call the Four Ds:

- Death
- Disease
- Divorce
- Disaster

I know it's morbid, and I would be the first one on board if people did not have to go through these experiences. But these are the facts of life.

I have encountered these challenges. If someone had helped me out when my family was facing medical difficulties and foreclosure, maybe I would not be where I am today. But having gone through those hard times also gives me compassion as a buyer. I know what it's like to be a motivated seller.

When people are dealing with any of the Four Ds, they need an immediate solution to their problems. They do not have the time to look for a real estate agent, wait for a house to be listed on the market, wait for potential buyers to make offers,

"This is he," I said, and my chest swelled because no one called me Mr. Montelongo.

"I have a business proposition for you," she said. "But you have to make me a promise."

"Well, what's the proposition and the promise?" I said.

"I have a client whose house burned down," she said. "It's been six months, and she already has her claim check. But she only has enough money to pay off her mortgage and not enough for repairs. She was underinsured." The insurance agent paused. "Now she wants to sell her house."

I tried to stay calm. "What's the promise?" I said.

"I have another client who called me saying you showed up at her house while her house was still smoldering. She was very upset that somebody would do this. She gave me your business card," she said.

"The promise is that you will not show up at people's houses like that again," she continued. "It's not the right time, and it takes four to six months for people to get their claims checks, anyway. What you're trying is not going to work."

It made sense to me. So I agreed: "In exchange for the information of the woman who settled her fire claim, I will never chase another fire truck."

## Lisa's Story

The insurance agent gave me her client's contact information. Lisa had already settled with the insurance company and received her check the day before. That's when I called her.

wait for a property to close and wait to get paid. They need a solution now.

Motivated sellers are often willing to sell their houses at deep discounts in exchange for an immediate sale. A lot of times, the solution they need is not price.

You can find motivated sellers in many different ways: through insurance lawyers, real estate agents and bail bondsmen, to name a few. I will explain more about these sources in the next two chapters.

### How to Negotiate with Homeowners

Once you have found a motivated seller, you need to solve their problem first. You find out what the problem is by simply asking and listening. That's negotiation.

In fact, most negotiation consists of simply listening. Listening builds rapport, trust and emotional investment. Just by listening, you will find out everything needed to close the deal. Listening allows you to find out what a homeowner really needs. Often, a homeowner's true needs have nothing to do with the house itself.

When you can solve a homeowner's problems, you are more likely to seal the deal and then solve your own problems.

Here is a step-by-step guide for how to interact with homeowners. You can use variations of the same technique.

We talked on the phone for about 40 minutes.

In that time, Lisa told me the story of her life in that house. She had bought it for $78,000 many years ago and raised her son there. He had gotten sick and she nursed him back to health in that house. She had divorced her first husband, but kept the house. Then she married her second husband in the house. All their friends came for the party, drank too much and threw glitter and rice everywhere. It took two weeks to get all the glitter and rice out of the carpet. Her son graduated from high school and went to college. He partied too much in college and started racking up student loans. He wanted to be a doctor, but was behind on loans.

I just listened.

Lisa then talked about the day when she went to buy clothes for her son. She had left a candle burning in the house. The candle flame caught the drapes and the fire spread to the kitchen, then whipped the ceiling. The air conditioner was on that day and sucked fire through the whole house. She told me the fire spread because the builder had not used the right materials and how the whole house was up in flames by the time the firefighters arrived.

I kept listening.

Lisa then explained how the insurance company was a hassle to deal with. They took forever to process the claims. She went around and around to get her money, and in the end, they did not pay her enough. They put her up in another house while they settled the claims, but she still had to make her mortgage payments. Meanwhile, her son had gotten even more behind on his student loans. She was underinsured and did not have enough equity in her house. She owed around $80,000 on the mortgage. Even worse, the insurance company penalized her for being underinsured and only gave her $80,000 for her entire claim, but it would cost an additional $60,000

## Steps for Talking to Homeowners

1. **Prepare**

   a. Research the property. Know your facts before you meet the seller. Look on the county records Web site to find out the square footage of the property. Find sales comparable with the property. This will give you the market price or after-repair value. This way, when you are on site, all you will need to do is assess the repairs.

   b. Take paperwork. Have a purchase package ready, including real estate contract, authorization for mortgage information, etc. Leave the paperwork in the car when you meet the homeowner; you need to seem friendly, not like you're going to take the property.

   c. Take a camera. You want to take pictures, especially if you will be doing a short sale – asking the bank for a discount on the loan.

   d. Pack your smile. People will sell to friendly people.

2. **Meet the Homeowner**

   a. Introduce yourself. Do not give a business card at this point; it's too distracting. You want the seller to focus on you, not look at paper.

for repairs. She was so frustrated because no one would give her a loan for repairs and she was stuck with a burned house. She was so angry she wanted to sue the insurance company for not insuring her properly, but she did not want to wait two more years to obtain more money and rebuild the house.

Finally, Lisa seemed to be done.

I asked her, "What can I do to help you?"

"I need to sell the house and pay off my son's student loans," she said.

"How much are your son's student loans?" I asked.

"Well, my son has $6,000 in student loans," she said.

"If I pay off your son's $6,000 in loans, will you give me the house?" I asked.

"Yes," she said.

"I'll buy it."

The words just tumbled out of my mouth. As soon as I said it, I thought to myself, "What the hell did I just say?"

I thought to myself: "Wow, I have my first deal. But I don't have any money. What am I going to do? I will find a way to make it work!"

**Finding the Money**

After I talked to Lisa, I went to see the house. It was 70 percent burned down. The Fire Department had boarded up the front door.

3.  **Build Rapport**

    a. Listen.

    b. Address a homeowner by first name. People love hearing the sound of their own name more than anything else.

    c. Mirror their speech. If the homeowner talks quickly, you want to talk quickly. If he or she is very calm, you want to be calm. If he or she is very solemn or even depressed, speak quietly.

    d. Be empathetic. You are here to solve the homeowner's problem. You will never get a deal without solving the problem. You can only do so if you have empathy.

4.  **Assess Repairs**

    a. Say to the homeowner: "Tell me about the property." This gives the seller the opportunity to walk you through the property and talk about their problems. The longer you let homeowners talk about their problems without interruption, the more they remember why they want to sell the property.

    b. Never call it their "home." Always call it "the property." This helps the seller emotionally detach from the property.

    c. Fill out your budget sheet. This is when you assess the amount of repair work the property will need. Budget sheets for repairs are provided in my Flip and Grow Rich programs.

There were four standing exterior rocks walls, but everything inside was gone. There were no interior walls, no drywall, no roof, no ceiling. There were toilets and tubs, but all the furniture was burned and everything else was soot. It smelled like a barbecue. The swimming pool was the only thing in good shape.

I looked up the property value on the county records. The land alone was worth $10,000. I did not know much about real estate back then, but I figured I could not go wrong with the price.

The next day, Lisa called. "It turns out my son has $9,000 in student loans," she said.

I did not know if it was actually true or not, but I was incensed. I did not like that she was trying to change the deal on me, and I almost walked away.

However, I thought to myself, "This might just be the golden opportunity I need."

"OK, I'll pay you $9,000 for it," I said.

After that, my mind went nuts. I thought, "How am I going to get the money? How will I pay for this?"

I had to borrow the money. I persuaded a friend of a friend of a friend to loan me the money. I tried to borrow the full $9,000 at first but could get only $2,500. I promised the person I would pay him $1,000 in interest in six to eight weeks – so he would get paid back $3,500. I was able to repay him in three weeks.

That night, I met Lisa at her rented house and signed the contract. I had typed up a rough contract using a borrowed computer. I gave her a check for $2,500 and promised to pay her the balance after I sold the house.

    d. Subtract the total repair costs to determine how much to pay, using the 70 Percent Rule. This formula is explained in a later chapter.

    e. Now you have your offer amount.

5. **Ask Questions**

    a. Once the seller has stopped talking, ask questions.

    b. Always find out what a homeowner wants.

    c. Never tell a homeowner what you want.

    d. Ask, "What is the problem?" This is the most important question you can ask. Even if the homeowner has already told you, ask this question anyway. Homeowners won't think you didn't listen; on the contrary, they will feel that you truly care.

    e. Ask, "Why are you selling the property?" Homeowners nearly always will tell you why. Remember, why they are selling the property forms the heart and soul of your negotiations later.

    f. Ask, "How far behind are you on payments?" and "Are you behind on property taxes? If so, how much?" The answers to these last two questions tell you how much room you have for negotiation later.

    g. Ask the "hero" question: "How is it that I can ultimately help you?" This is where you step in to solve the homeowner's problems. You will be shocked how often homeowners tell you, "Just take the property off of my hands!"

Looking back, I realize how little I knew. I didn't go through a title or escrow company – I didn't even know what those were. It was not until later that I learned that buyers usually give the down payment to a title company so that sellers do not run off with the money.

But that night, I walked out of Lisa's house feeling on top of the world. I was excited and full of hope.

## Selling the Property

Next, I contacted a real estate agent and explained that I had a property with a burned house I would like to sell. I told him the land value alone was worth $10,000 and the house still had good walls, a solid foundation, intact plumbing and a pool. I figured there must be enough additional value in the house where I could make a profit. I had also called a plumber and had him assess the plumbing for me at no charge.

I listed the property with a real estate agent. It sold for $27,000 and closed in two weeks. Later, I learned that the transaction was called a "double close."

But I did not know at the time how to do any kind of closing. I called a title company and said, "I need to sell a property. How do I do it?" I sat on the phone for 45 minutes with a closing officer and had her explain how the process works because I had no clue. She was really wonderful about taking me through the ABCs of it. Because she took that time with me, she won my loyalty. To this day, she closes the vast majority of my deals.

The new buyer, who was a rehabber, came in and paid me $27,000 for the property. I had tripled the amount of money I paid for it. After the property closed, I gave the new buyer the plumber's phone

6. **Make Offer**

   a. Readdress the seller by name.

   b. Let him or her know the cost of repairs using a general contractor. This amount is typically 50 percent more than your cost. So if your repair costs add up to $20,000, a general contractor will charge $30,000. Do not tell the homeowner how much it will cost you – say how much it will cost them using a general contractor.

   c. Make offer.

7. **Negotiate if Necessary**

   a. If the homeowner is stuck on a sales price that will not allow you to hit the 70 Percent Rule, knowing how many payments they have missed and how close they are to foreclosure gives you emotional leverage.

   b. Aim to create a win-win situation, so that the homeowner's problem is solved, while you have a price that meets the lenders requirements.

   c. Repeat the homeowner's name.

   d. Kindly ask: "Why are you selling this property?" This will remind the homeowner of why the house is for sale.

   e. Kindly remind the homeowner of all the challenges in the property.

   f. Remind the homeowner how much the repairs will cost out-of-pocket to hire a general contractor.

number and bid, to use as the buyer saw fit. He fixed the house and eventually sold it for about $140,000.

With my profit, I gave the original homeowner the balance of $6,500, and kept the remaining $18,000.

Next, I paid off one of my most important liabilities: the $1,000 I borrowed from my dad to move across the country. I offered to pay him interest, but he declined the interest. He said he was just glad that I was able to start taking care of my family.

What a terrific return on my investment, which was $2,500. But, in fact, I had invested zero in the property because the $2,500 was borrowed. I paid back the $2,500 with interest, and everybody won.

I was hooked! I knew that this was what I had to do. I took the money and wanted to grow my business. I began talking to lawyers who sue insurance companies. I had gotten this small idea from the woman who sold me Lisa's property. However, it opened my eyes to a bigger opportunity.

g. Explain that in order to save the homeowner from foreclosure, the price needs to be closer to the pay-off amount.

h. Ask, "If I can solve this problem in the next 14 days, and you never have to think about it again, would you sell it to me for 'X' price?"

8. **Shut Up**

a. Once a homeowner agrees to sell the property, shut up! Don't talk yourself out of a deal.

b. Keep listening. Do not talk too much.

c. When appropriate, ask the homeowner to "authorize the paperwork." Never ask to "sign a contract."

d. Get the paperwork from your car.

e. Sign the contracts.

You want to create a win-win situation. Your goal in negotiation is to meet the seller's emotional and/or financial needs, while also meeting your need of buying at the 70 Percent Rule. This is the only way you will be able to qualify for a loan on this type of investment. You do not want to solve the homeowner's problems, then be stuck without a loan later.

When signing the contract, it is much easier for people to "authorize a sale," which puts them in control, than to "sign a contract," which can make them feel trapped. This will make the seller trust you more. Also, technically, it is not a contract until both sides sign the papers.

# Chapter 8

## The Next Deal
*Learning from Lawyers*

- **Looking for Deals**
- **Solving Attorneys' Problems**
- **The Expert Witness Deal**
- **Splitting Costs**

## Looking for Deals

After my first deal, I was eager to do more.

I had to make more money. Even though I was able to make my first month's rent, the next month's rent was coming up fast. The $15,000 I made on the first deal, after paying off real estate agent commissions, was the largest amount of money I had ever made. But I knew it would quickly run out over the next few months.

So I began to look for more deals. I wanted to do another quick flip in the next two months – three months at most. I thought about the woman whose house I had purchased. She was really angry at the insurance company and talked about suing the company for underinsuring her. I figured there had to be other people who are suing insurance companies.

To find them, I passed my business cards to insurance agents throughout town. I told everyone that I bought burned houses. But

After you have left the house, sellers occasionally attempt to get out of a contract for various reasons. Typically, I have found that the real reason is because another investor offered a higher price. Even if you offer to match that price, the homeowner usually declines, because he or she is too embarrassed to admit trying to weasel out of a deal.

Yes, I understand that you may feel the homeowner is entitled to a higher price. However, when a seller has already entered into a legal and binding agreement, you need to fight for what is right. Let them know they are under contract and hold them to it.

In my Flip and Grow Rich program, I teach you how to legally keep tens of thousands of dollars in your pocket for less than $20 by having the proper paperwork in place. In situations where a real estate contract might otherwise fall apart, the right paperwork typically makes me an additional $40,000 per year.

### WIIFM Radio

Remember that people listen only to WIIFM Radio – "What's in it for me?"

Do not make the mistake of saying, "This doesn't work for me" or "I don't want to waste your time or my time."

Remember, sellers only care about what's in it for them. They don't care how much you know about construction, mortgage loans, interest rates or how much the house is worth. They care about how much you care about helping them get out of their situation.

agents told me that when people's houses burned down, they contact a claims adjuster directly and most insurance agents would never know when the property had a loss. Once in a while, the agents would get complaints, but they didn't handle it.

Then I went back to the insurance agent who told me about the first deal I did. She said that it was extremely unusual that two of her clients had contacted her about their burned houses. Usually, the homeowners deal with the claims departments. Then she gave me the contact for the claims department in her company.

But when I called the claims department, I got nowhere. After making a lot of calls, I found out that large insurance corporations often farm out work to local claims adjustment companies. This happens when there are a lot of claims, such as after a hailstorm.

Next, I started talking to individual claims adjusters. One older woman was very friendly and helpful. "If you don't mind," I said, "I'd love to take you out to lunch and pick your brain so I can learn from you."

She said yes.

As we settled down at a casual restaurant, I started asking questions. I asked her about the claims process; how people get insurance; what people do when their houses burn down; what happens if they're underinsured; and how they handle the claims.

She told me that most people with burned houses just want to settle, fix their house and move on. Most people do not sell their houses. I was stumped. Then I asked, "Don't you sometimes have people who are upset?"

"Yes," she said. She leaned closer to me. "It's not in my best interest to tell you this, but there are people who sue us because we either

If homeowners see that you're just in this for the money, they will never sell you their property. If they think that you're there to help them out, you've got a deal.

underinsure them or they hire attorneys who find loopholes in their insurance policies."

Now I was getting somewhere.

Then she said slowly, "If you go after attorneys, you will find the people who are in insurance lawsuits."

BAM! "That's how to find motivated sellers," I thought.

Then she promised to help. "Let me give you the names of the attorneys in town," she said.


## Solving Attorneys' Problems

The next day, I started contacting those insurance attorneys. I wrote a letter, which basically said, "Hi, I would like to help you settle your insurance lawsuits. If you have people who are upset with their insurance claims, I can help."

I figured that if I could help attorneys solve their problems, they would want to do business with me. I even walked into a few attorneys' offices, telling them I could help. Unfortunately, no one responded.

By now, it had been four months since my first deal closed, and I was running out of money. I needed to support my family, and I had deadlines to meet. I needed to flip a house in the next 90 days.

Then I got a phone call from an attorney.

"I have a client who is in a lawsuit," he said. A couple lived in the house, and the house was molded over, he explained. "If you can assess the property and tell me what it's worth, I can use you."

# Chapter H

## Deals from Attorneys
Buying Homes from Homeowners with Insurance Claims

- **Find Insurance Lawyers**
- **Why Homeowners Sue**
- **How Settlements Work**
- **The Expert Witness' Role**
- **How Homeowners Can Profit**
- **How Homeowners Use Settlements**
- **Sample Letter to Lawyer**

### Find Insurance Lawyers

One great way to find motivated sellers is to work with lawyers specializing in insurance cases. These lawyers often represent homeowners whose houses have construction problems and are suing their insurance companies for not reimbursing them enough money to cover the repair costs.

When you can solve these attorneys' problems, they will help solve your problems. You can solve these attorneys' problems by serving as an expert witness in real estate. They will help you by introducing you to their clients, who are frustrated and want to dump their houses. These are motivated sellers with undervalued homes.

Then he added, "One thing I need to know. Are you an expert in this field?"

I froze. I thought, "How am I going to be an expert and go up against these big attorneys?" Then I had another BAM! I realized that what these attorneys needed was an expert witness.

That's why I wasn't getting any phone calls. I thought about the first woman whose house had burned down. I thought about her lawyer. I thought about how he had needed an expert report. That's how I could help solve his problem – by becoming an expert witness.

"Sure, I'm an expert," I told the attorney on the phone.

"How much do you charge?" he asked.

"How much do you pay?" I said.

"We don't like to pay more than $100 an hour," he said.

"I'll tell you what," I said. "I'll go inspect the property at no charge. I will let you know what it is worth, and in return, I would like to talk to your client about the problem."

We had a deal.

That's when I realized that I didn't have to be lucky. Now, I could get deal after deal by solving lawyer problem after lawyer problem. I knew I had hit on something. I needed to be a problem-solver. When I solved other people's problems, I got deals. Now, with everyone I met, I would ask: "How can I help you solve your problem?"

Homeowners involved in insurance claims are often willing to sell at steep discounts because they are emotionally and financially exhausted. By the time you meet them, they have typically spent two years in litigation and want to move on with their lives. They want to take their settlement money and buy a new house. They don't want their old houses anymore.

## Why Homeowners Sue

Here's a more detailed breakdown of what happens when homeowners sue an insurance company. Most people who sue insurance companies have lived in their houses for decades. They have an emotional investment in their houses. By this time, they also have paid down a lot of the mortgage.

Then something bad happens, such as a fire or hailstorm. The house is destroyed. But they find out that the insurance company has underinsured them, and the money is not enough to cover the cost of repairs needed on the house.

Let's say a house is worth $350,000 and the mortgage balance is $250,000. If it is improperly insured or underinsured for $300,000, and the house needs $150,000 in repairs, that additional $100,000 that the insurance company did not properly insure can create a very motivated seller.

The homeowners are angry that they cannot get their old house back. And they are angry at the insurance company for not paying enough for repairs or underinsuring them. That's when they go to a lawyer to sue the insurance company.

If the homeowners have not lived in a house very long and have barely paid down the mortgage, they generally have very little

## The Expert Witness Deal

I met the attorney's clients at their house. Martin and Jessica were suing the insurance company for denying a claim for fixing the mold problem in the house.

Martin was a mild man. He spoke in short, quick sentences and was the more financially concerned of the two. Jessica was very conversational. They had been married for several years and had no children.

When I met Martin and Jessica, the first thing I asked was, "What's the problem?"

They talked for nearly three hours, telling me about when they bought the house, how the mold problem arose and how they later filed an insurance claim. They told me about all their problems up to the time I was now standing in the house.

They told me how the insurance company said that the mold problem wasn't major and that it would pay $5,000 for their claim.

Martin and Jessica were suing their insurance company. They had been fighting this battle for two years.

When they finished, I asked them, "How can I solve your problem?"

"Buy this house," said Martin.

So that's what I did.

Later, Martin and Jessica told me that they had talked to several real estate investors. But those investors were only interested in how much they wanted for the house. Those investors weren't interested in them as people.

vested interest. If the insurance company does not cover the repair costs, homeowners tend to accept the insured amount or simply let it go into foreclosure.

## How Settlements Work

If the homeowners decide to sue the insurance company, the lawsuit typically drags on for two years. This is because insurance companies try to bleed the homeowners dry. The insurance company may cut off the homeowners' additional living expenses, used to pay for other living quarters. The homeowners may have moved to another place because their home is so badly damaged, and they may be paying hotel fees or making payments on two places.

The attorney is gunning to win enough money to pay the mortgage and fix the house to bring up the value so the homeowners do not lose any money. The attorney determines a settlement amount that includes the loan balance or the value of the house, plus the cost of repairs, plus emotional damages.

Let's say the house needs $100,000 to $150,000 in repairs. The homeowners will get a quote from the most expensive contractor in town, say, $150,000. The lawyer will use that estimate in the lawsuit. In addition, the homeowners have not lived in the house for two years. At $3,500 in mortgage payments and rent or hotel fees a month – multiplied by two years – that's another $100,000 in damages. Add to that pain and suffering, plus breach of contract, and the lawyer can sue for $300,000 to $900,000.

But they liked me because I had listened to them.

So I bought their house for $45,000. It was worth $125,000 fixed up. Yes, I got it at 36 percent of the market value.

By the time Martin and Jessica met me, they were tired of fighting the insurance company. They just wanted to unload the house.

I solved their problem by buying their nightmare. The couple told their attorney: "That man was so nice. He actually helped us."


## Splitting Costs

Even though I was learning a lot about insurance claims and settlements at the time, I still had to figure out a way to make Martin and Jessica's deal turn into profits for myself. I had gotten a great deal on their house. But I was still cash-strapped.

Martin and Jessica had a bid from a general contractor for $50,000 in repairs. I knew I could do it for less than $30,000. But that wasn't money I had sitting around.

How was I going to pull this off? This was only my second deal, and I didn't know then what I do now. I needed to move quickly. I needed to flip this house as quickly as possible to feed my family.

I came up with a way to make it work. I decided to find someone who wanted to earn a great return on money. In exchange, I would provide the deal and oversee the project.

I called a businessman I had met while looking for insurance agents to give me deals. Doug had money to invest in real estate, but he didn't know where to find good deals. When I called Doug about this deal, I offered to split the profits if he provided the money to buy

Insurance companies want to avoid such cases going to jury trial, because the juries are made up of "peers" – which in this case means other homeowners. There is no such thing as a jury consisting of other multibillion-dollar insurance companies. The insurance companies know they will almost always lose if the case goes to trial, so they will settle out of court, offering a reduced amount on the lawsuit charges.

In this case, it would settle at maybe $600,000. The lawyer is typically paid 33 percent of the settlement, or nearly $200,000, leaving the homeowners with about $400,000 in cash. After selling the old house, the homeowners usually have enough cash from the settlement and house sale to pay off the current mortgage and buy a new house.

## The Expert Witness' Role

In order to determine the value of a house, the attorney calls in expert witnesses to value the home. The expert witness is not a licensed home inspector or appraiser. He or she is simply a potential home buyer or investor who says how much he or she is willing to pay for the home in its present condition.

Just about anyone can become an expert witness, including you. The term "expert witness" does not mean you are an expert. It just means that you can serve as a witness for the lawyer with your devalued house bid. If "X" amount is the maximum amount you are willing to pay, and the attorney cannot find anybody else who is willing to pay more than that, the attorney can use you in a court of law as an expert witness.

the house and pay for repairs. He asked what rate of return I offered. I said I would give him a generous fifty percent of the profits. He quickly agreed.

Meanwhile, I was personally stretched. I needed to complete this flip as quickly as possible, because I was running low on cash and had bills due.

I fixed the house for $27,000 and put it up for sale. Then I found a buyer. We had listed the house dramatically under market. It was a $125,000 house, priced at $105,000, or 15 percent off. By selling at a huge discount, I knew I could turn this flip quickly. The house was under contract in a week.

That taught me a valuable lesson. Although I really wanted to make the extra profit by selling it at full market value, by not being greedy I was able to flip the property quickly. That helped build my cash reserves.

I used those profits to catapult my business. I quickly secured two more properties. Most people believe that the money partner is in a position of power. However, I believe I was in a position of power, because I was able to take that $16,500 and acquire two more properties to flip.

I did one of those flips with a partner and the other by myself. Thus, I was able to expand my empire because I increased the number of flips I was doing. Had I waited around for top dollar, the next two deals might have been gone by the time I sold this one.

The fact that you're offering to buy that house at a certain price makes you a real estate investor, whether or not you've ever purchased real estate.

The "testimony" is usually a piece of paper saying how much the investor thinks the house is worth and why.

The expert witness is typically needed not long before the settlement is paid – anywhere from two weeks to a few months. This is because the lawyer wants as current a market value as possible. If the lawyer calls an investor too early in the case, the value may be different.

By this time, the homeowners are exhausted. They just want to move on. Typically, what they say is: "We don't want the house back. It's a nightmare. If we get a good settlement, we want to pay off the mortgage and buy a new house."

That's when the expert witness and investor has the opportunity to make an offer to the homeowner. By doing so, the investor is helping to solve the homeowners' problems by unburdening them from a house that has caused so much emotional pain. It becomes a win-win solution.

# Chapter 9

## Honing My Skills
### *The Basics of My Business*

- **Learning Experiences**
- **Jail and Bail**
- **Show Me the Money**
- **Mastermind Group**
- **The New Goal**

## Learning Experiences

I made a lot of mistakes in those early deals. But those mistakes helped me hone my skills as a real estate investor.

I learned not to overdo it on the flips. If I make every room fancy, I would kill my budget. My flips need to be around a "9" of beauty – not "10." If I go to a 10, I start losing money.

In early 2002, I bought a fire-damaged house. It was such an easy flip, I did not make it a priority to get done – so the contractors did not make it a priority. They tore out the cabinets and let them sit. They did some paint work and did not finish the job. The contractors took their time and soon lost interest. I had to fire them and hire new contractors. The job took an additional six weeks to finish, which is too long.

# How the Homeowners' Problem is Solved

### After disaster

**House**

| Market value (fixed up) | = | $350,000 |
|---|---|---|
| Homeowners' mortgage | = − | $250,000 |
| Repairs needed | = − | $150,000 |
| Insurance coverage | = + | $300,000 |
| Homeowners' shortfall | = − | $100,000 |

### After settlement

**Insurance Company**

| Settlement | = + $600,000 |
|---|---|

**Homeowners**

| Settlement funds | = | + $400,000 |
|---|---|---|
| House sale | = | + $145,000 |
| Total income | = | + $545,000 |
| Mortgage payoff | = | − $250,000 |
| Profit | = | + $295,000 |

**Lawyer**

| Lawsuit | = | + $900,000 |
|---|---|---|
| Settlement | = | + $600,000 |
| Homeowners' funds | = | − $400,000 |
| Earnings | = | + $200,000 |

**Bank**

| Mortgage owed | = | − $250,000 |
|---|---|---|
| Mortgage payoff | = | + $250,000 |
| Balance | = | $0 |

**Flipper**

| House purchase | = | − $145,000 |
|---|---|---|
| Repairs | = | − $100,000 |
| Total cost (= 70% market value) | = | − $245,000 |
| Market value | = | + $350,000 |
| Potential profit | = | + $105,000 |

That house was worth $150,000 fixed up. I had bought it for $60,000. The repair costs were $20,000. But because I let it sit so long, it cost an additional $4,300 in interest and $10,000 more in repairs. I still made a good profit. But I lost $14,300 because of delays.

After that, I made schedules for contractors. I also implemented a penalty fee of $75 for each day the job goes past the deadline. That's not enough money to hurt contractors badly, but enough to motivate them to get the job done on time.

I also decided that I needed to get more educated. Over the next 18 months, I read hundreds of books. That education was very important in my understanding of the business. But there were still holes in the information, and as I grew my business, I learned to fill those holes and perfect my system.

## Jail and Bail

One day, one of my contractors didn't show up for work. This was very unlike him. He didn't show up the next day, either. Then I got a phone call from him around 11 p.m.

"Hey, Armando," he said. "Can you post bail for me? I'm in jail."

"What happened?" I asked.

"Aw, you know, I just got into a little scuffle," he said. "This guy pushed me around, you know."

"I don't know how to post bail," I said.

"You gotta go to a bail bondsman," he said.

I wasn't really interested in bailing out this guy. I figured that if he

## How Homeowners Can Profit

Over the years, I have learned how homeowners can sell their houses after receiving their settlement checks, regardless of the mortgage balance.

Usually, my price to the owners is more than the mortgage amount. So when the house closes, the entire mortgage is paid off and the homeowners walk away with some profit.

For example, if a house is worth $500,000 and it needs $100,000 in repairs, I need to buy the house for $250,000 to make a profit. That's my offer price.

In most cases, the mortgage owed is less than my offer price. If they accept my offer, they make a profit on the difference. Let's say the mortgage owed is $200,000. After selling the house to me for $250,000, the homeowners pay off the mortgage and keep the extra $50,000. They can use this profit, plus the settlement check of $200,000, to buy a new house.

In some cases, the mortgage balance is more than my offer price. In this case, the homeowners can use part of the settlement money to make up the difference. Let's say the mortgage in this case is $300,000, but I can buy it only for $250,000. The homeowners can take $50,000 of their $200,000 settlement money to make up the difference and walk away. That still leaves them $150,000 of settlement money to buy a new house.

In all cases, the homeowners are free to move on.

was a big enough boy to get into trouble, he was a big enough boy to get out of trouble.

But I was curious to see what he was really in jail for. So the next day, I called the bail bondsman, and spoke with his secretary.

She explained that she could not give out that information, so out of curiosity I asked her how the bail system works. She explained that many people use a bail bondsman to post bail.

"What if someone does not have the money to pay you back?" I asked.

She explained that the person in jail uses their house as collateral. The bail bondsman takes a lien against the house to secure their interest.

In this case, my contractor who called me for help hoped I would pay his bail or use one of my houses as a guarantee to the bail bondsman. I had no intention of doing that, but my interest was piqued as to how this whole process worked.

"So what exactly would I do?" I asked.

"You become the guarantor for the loan," said the bail bondsmen's secretary.

"Well, what happens if the guy jumps bail?" I asked.

"We get a judgment against your house."

I thought, "There must be tons of people out there who jump bail." I watched it on TV all the time: bad guy gets arrested, bad guy goes to jail, bad guy jumps bail. I smelled opportunity.

Because the expert witness is always called shortly before the settlement takes place, it means that I never have to wait two years to get the house.

## How Homeowners Use Settlements

The homeowner has several options, depending on how much mortgage is owed. Here's one example.

House value after repairs: $500,000

Repair cost: $100,000

Price investor will pay: $250,000

Settlement amount: $200,000

|  | Case 1 | Case 2 | Case 3 |
|---|---|---|---|
| **Mortgage balance** | $200,000 | $250,000 | $300,000 |
| **Homeowners' action** | Sell house for $250,000 | Sell house for $250,000 | Sell house for $250,000 |
|  | * pay off mortgage | * pay off mortgage | * pay off mortgage with $250,000 from house sale and $50,000 from settlement |
|  | * make $50,000 profit | * make $0 profit |  |
|  | * use settlement and profit to buy new house | * use settlement to buy new house | * use remaining $150,000 of settlement to buy new house |

"Wow," I said. "Do you ever have guys who don't pay?"

"All the time," she said.

"What do you do?"

"We sue them," she said.

"Then what do you do?"

"If we win the lawsuit, we get a judgment against them," she said. "If they don't pay on the judgment, we file a lien on their property and foreclose."

I smelled more opportunity.

"What happens after you foreclose?" I asked.

"Well, I don't know," she said. "That's one of my boss's gripes."

More opportunity! "What does your boss do with the houses?" I asked.

"Well," she said, "he usually gets property that's really beat up, and he doesn't really want them. But it's his only recourse."

That's how I could help solve their problems! The next day, I started calling bail bondsmen.

What happened to the contractor? I don't know. After talking on the phone for a while, the secretary disclosed that the contractor actually had assaulted his girlfriend. He had lied to me and committed a terrible crime. I never hired him again.

But I started picking up properties from bail bondsmen.

By working with lawyers and homeowners who are settling insurance claims, you have the opportunity to serve as an expert witness and unload homes, so the homeowners are free to move on. That's what is great about being a house flipper. You get to solve people's problems while making a profit.

### Sample Letter to Lawyer

You can contact insurance lawyers by sending out letters. Here is a sample.

> *Dear Lawyer:*
>
> *My name is Happy Flipper. I understand you may be in need of having an expert witness for any real-estate-related cases. I am happy to be an expert witness for you for ZERO DOLLARS. Contact me if you are suing a builder or an insurance company, have someone in divorce, bankruptcy or foreclosure, and you need an expert witness to assess the property quickly and for free. Please call me at (your phone number).*
>
> *Sincerely,*
> *Happy Flipper*

## Show Me the Money

During that time, I learned about two key things from my mentors that still form the financial foundation of my business today: the 70 Percent Rule and hard-money lenders.

The 70 Percent Rule gave me a formula for how much to buy my houses. It told me how much to allow for profit, overhead and other expenses so that I did not have to buy the property with any of my own money. It also showed me a way to roll monthly payments into the loan. Basically, the rule told me to buy a house at 70 percent of the fixed-up value, minus repair costs.

Hard-money lenders are the epitome of using "other people's money" to create your wealth – a principle my mentors always stressed. It gave me a way to fund the deals I found. I learned what these lenders want, how they are different from banks, how they work and how to use them. While banks lend you money based on your credit, hard-money lenders lend you money based on the deal.

Working with hard-money lenders, I had the confidence to buy all the deals I could find. I could honestly say to anyone: "I literally have half a million dollars burning a hole in my pocket."

More importantly, I saw how true wealth is created. You can have a job making a salary. You can be a business owner making an income. You can be an investor using your own money. Or you can get wealthy using other people's money. That's what I wanted.

By using other people's money, I realized that my returns on investment were infinite. This meant that I could secure a deal with zero dollars of my own money invested, but I could make tens of thousands of dollars in profits. That makes my return on investment infinite.

# Chapter I

## More Ways to Find Deals
Create a System for Leads

- **Business Systems**
- **Foreclosures**
- **Short Sales**
- **REO Real Estate Agents**
- **Bail Bondsmen**
- **Finding Systems**

### Business Systems

I have created a Flip and Grow Rich system. It's a well-oiled machine, similar to how Henry Ford created a system to build cars. It's a system of strategies to buy houses. I took something that most people find difficult and made it extremely easy.

I flip a lot of houses, but I don't walk around stressed and freaking out every day. I actually have time on my hands. That's because my system is set up to do the work. I do not have to work hard. I work smart.

I define a system as a series of organized strategies. I've organized these strategies in the way that the alphabet is organized: from A to Z.

## Mastermind Group

After doing several flips and making money, I felt that something else was missing. I realized I needed that consistent reinforcement. I needed an environment of empowerment.

Some of my old friends from childhood were working at salaried jobs. When I talked about the deals and profits I made, some of them were supportive, but many just smiled and changed the subject. Looking back, I can see that many friends and family could not be supportive because they did not have a positive psychology of money.

Some family members also were skeptical. They thought real estate investing was really risky. They told me to be responsible and get a steady job.

I knew I was on the right track. But I needed to create an environment of empowerment around me. It may sound weird, but I decided to do something that was suggested in that classic wealth book, *Think and Grow Rich*, by Napoleon Hill.

Hill wrote about creating a "mastermind group," a group of individuals who support your success. Well, at the time, I didn't know who to invite to be in such a group. So I decided to make one up. I cut out pictures and put them on a board in my office.

The members of my mastermind group were Warren Buffet, because he is a savvy investor; Donald Trump, for being in real estate; Richard Branson, for his ability to be adventurous and have fun; Bill Gates, for his innovation; Anthony Robbins, for encouraging continual education; and my dad, for being honest and a good family man.

At night, I looked at my mastermind group. When I was discouraged, I thought about what they would do. When I was

My Flip and Grow Rich system gives you strategies for finding deals and money, hiring and managing contractors, selling houses and making your money safe.

You want your system to bring deals to you. You don't have to work hard looking for deals. I much prefer smart work to hard work.

Set up your system to have several ways of finding deals. Working with attorneys who sue insurance companies and builders is a great strategy. However, if you want an abundant supply of deals, you need a systematic way of having motivated sellers come to you.

You never want to be locked into only a few ways of finding deals. The more you have people sending you deals, the less you have to work at chasing the dollar. That's how you work smart.

**Foreclosures**

People who face foreclosure can use help from investors.

You can find homeowners facing foreclosure in several ways, including:

1. County records – The county releases lists of homeowners who are in default of their mortgage loans. In this case, the banks are foreclosing on them.

2. County tax assessor – The tax assessor releases lists of homeowners who have not paid property taxes for a length of time. The county is foreclosing on the property.

challenged, I talked to them. They created positive peer pressure for me. They raised the bar for possibility. They helped create an environment of empowerment around me.

## The New Goal

In 2002, I met a few other rehabbers at a seminar. We were just a few people standing at the back of the room, chatting casually.

These guys had been rehabbing houses for many years. These rehabbers were very proud of what they did and spoke very confidently about how they were among the best in the business.

I was interested in what they had to say because I thought I could learn something. I felt like the new kid on the block just trying to find my way in the business. At the time, I had been in the business for a little more than a year. But I was proud of myself for having worked my way from living in a garage to supporting my family.

I tried not to show my nervousness. I casually asked, "So how many houses do you flip a month?"

"Two or three," one guy said.

Another said, "Three or four in a good month, but usually around three."

Then they asked how many I did a month. Well, by now, I was working consistently and had scored a particularly good month.

"Three to four," I said, unsure of myself. "But this month, I did six."

Their jaws dropped.

3. Competitors – Competitors sometimes refer homeowners who are in foreclosure. For various reasons, these competitors do not want to do the deal. Typically, such a person earns a referral fee when a deal closes.

4. Mail – Homeowners respond to fliers sent through the mail.

It would have relieved so much stress if an investor bought my property while I was in foreclosure.

The truth is tens of thousands of people are out there facing foreclosure right now and they don't know that an investor can help. It's our job to relieve that stress from people, and then we turn safe profits.

After being on both sides of foreclosure, I know that this business really does help motivated sellers.

### Short Sales

Short sales with banks are another way to negotiate great deals.

Maybe you will walk into a property, and it does not have enough equity for the homeowner to sell at a good price. Equity is the difference between the property's market value and what is owed on the house. In this case, the homeowner owes more on the mortgage than the house is worth.

If you meet a homeowner who faces foreclosure, you can put the house under contract for less than the value of the mortgage, with the condition that the bank will forgive the existing loan – or a portion of it – and sell it at the contract price.

I was a little embarrassed. I felt like the kid who figured out the math problem that couldn't be solved, because no one had told me it couldn't be done.

Something went off in me. I felt a huge surge of motivation. I realized that if I could do six deals in a month, I could do more than 20 deals a month. That became my new big goal.

I thought to myself how rare it is that someone can be the best in their field, a leader in their industry. That's what I now wanted to do. It became an inspiration for me.

Then you make a deal with the bank to do a short sale. This means bringing down the price to the contract offer amount so there's enough room for you, the investor, to make a profit. The final deal is a contract with the bank.

This is another technique for buying properties at a discount. When the market is saturated with foreclosures, banks are much more motivated to negotiate.

Contact the bank's loss mitigation department and say you want to help them by purchasing properties that they have foreclosed on or are about to foreclose on. Each bank is different as to how they list and handle foreclosures, so this technique requires more time to get through the different bank channels.

**REO Real Estate Agents**

Real estate agents can also help you find houses.

But a lot of real estate agents do not know how to help investors. Some agents have wasted their time with uneducated investors and they don't want to risk that again. Other agents think that every house in foreclosure is a deal. That's not the case.

You want to work with real estate agents who specialize in real-estate owned, or REO, properties. These are houses owned by banks after people have gone through foreclosure.

REO houses are not always deals, either. But because an REO agent is representing the bank, they often give me the opportunity to negotiate strong deals.

# Chapter 10

## Multimillionaire Mentors
*Strategies for Long-Term Wealth*

- **Chasing Multimillionaires**
- **The Doctor Investor**
- **Speed of Cash Theory**
- **My $60,000 Mistake**

### Chasing Multimillionaires

I'm very bad at a lot of things. I'm not a great cook and I'm not an artist. But one thing I am good at is chasing down millionaires. It is hard to convince millionaires to go to lunch with you. But I did. And they all became my mentors.

Early in my career, I found four multimillionaire mentors. They were a doctor, a contractor, a business consultant and a blind man. All attained their wealth through real estate.

I picked their brains and listened to their advice. They helped me formulate my strategy for long-term wealth. They advised me on deals. And they taught me humility.

Some real estate agents can also give you access to the multiple-listing service, or MLS, in exchange for using them to broker your deals. This will enable you to do your own research, so you can compare market values of houses you are considering.

## Bail Bondsmen

Bail bondsmen are another great source for deals. They sometimes wind up with houses from people who have jumped bail. The real estate investor can help solve the bondsmen's problems by turning their unwanted houses into cash.

When someone goes to jail, that person can post bail to go free. Bail is typically 10 percent of the bond amount. So if it's a $50,000 bond, they have to post $5,000.

If the bail bondsman doesn't get repaid, he will go through the court process and file a judgment against the person who went to jail or someone who took out the bail loan on their behalf – typically a parent who owns real estate.

Then the bondsman will execute that judgment and acquire a lien against any real property owned by the parent. Now the bondsman has a judgment, and possibly the property, but no cash. This is where you come in and buy the property.

Another scenario is that the bondsman will take an up-front lien against a property – usually a house – to act as collateral against the bail.

## The Doctor Investor

One multimillionaire taught me about creating long-term wealth.

An associate introduced me to a sports medicine doctor named Greg, who had made his fortune through real estate investing. Greg always said his practice gave him a paycheck, but real estate gave him wealth.

"Wow," I thought to myself. "This guy has some serious dollars. I better get to know him and pick his brain." So I invited him to lunch at an upscale steak and seafood restaurant, not far from his medical office, in a posh part of town.

Greg was 70. He had a small build and a straight back. His hair was gray with golden-brown specks. He had a stern look and an intense gaze and wore round spectacles. He would smile once in a while, laugh a bit, and go right back to business.

Greg's medical office and home were in expensive districts, but he ran his real estate business from a small two-bedroom house in a run-down neighborhood. He did not need more than that, he said. He was a frugal man.

When we ordered, I ordered a steak, fish and shrimp meal. Greg asked for a small soup and a lettuce wedge. "That's what I like," he said. "It keeps my energy high."

"Doctor," I said, as we waited for the food to arrive, "I don't want to ask anything of you. I'm not asking for money or a free deal. I'm asking for your expertise. Tell me what I need to do in life to get wealthy."

He nodded.

"Armando, if you give people what they want, before you take what you want for yourself, you will become wealthy," he said.

**Finding Systems**

As you build your flipping business, you will want to have paperwork in place for finding deals. This helps you create a system, which generates business for you.

In my Flip and Grow Rich system, I have 14 standard letters for finding motivated sellers. These include letters to:

- homeowners with houses destroyed by fire
- insurance lawyers
- bail bondsmen
- pre-foreclosures
- vacant-property owners

When you have the systems in place for finding deals, you will not have to work as hard at chasing them. They will come to you.

"I'm flipping houses, and it's going well," I explained. "Some houses are really discounted. I'm buying these things 40 cents on the dollar. With repair costs, I'm in 50 cents to 60 cents on the dollar. I could put a renter in each house and make $200 or $300 a month. If I do that for 10 to 15 houses a month, that's at least $3,000 a month."

I continued, "I'm thinking down the road, this might be the way to go, to build long-term wealth."

"Well, $3,000 a month is fine," Greg said. "But you're a young man. You need to build cash reserves first. You need to do that before you start thinking about building residual income."

He continued: "If you have 10 houses, and you make $300 cash flow in rent for each house, that's $3,000 a month.

"But if you flip 10 houses a month, and you make $20,000 each deal, that's $200,000 a month. Now you're building big cash reserves."

Greg had started his career flipping houses. This gave him the capital he needed to buy and hold rental and commercial properties later. He owned more than 1,000 rental units and mortgage notes. He was also a major shareholder in a bank.

Greg also gave me a bigger vision for financial success. Greg practiced medicine without pay – he donated his time to help people who lacked money for medical services. This is the power that real estate can provide.

"You need to be worth $1 million to $5 million to be on the radar of the financial world," he said. "If you want to be in the top one percent of all America, you need to be at the $5 million mark or more."

I had a game plan. I would build my cash reserves first by flipping houses before going after long-term wealth with rental properties. I decided to save enough money to not have to work for two years before going into rental and commercial properties.

# Chapter J

## Where to Find Money
Tap into an Abundance of Investment Money

- **The Speed of Cash at Work**
- **How Much to Pay**
- **The 70 Percent Rule**
- **Hard-Money Lenders**
- **Private Investors**
- **Partners**
- **Funding Systems**

### The Speed of Cash at Work

Your ability to build wealth is directly related to the speed of cash. Most small businesses run across cash-flow problems. That is why I chose flipping houses. You can start with no money, but just as importantly, you can add large sums of cash to your bank account quickly.

Flipping houses enables you to increase your rate of building cash reserves. That's partly because the rate at which you make money flipping houses is typically higher than being employed.

## Speed of Cash Theory

After talking to Greg, I wanted to build cash reserves fast. Real estate investing is about the speed of cash. I realized that the faster I could get cash into my hands, the stronger the momentum would build for wealth. The faster I could build my cash reserves, the faster I could reinvest it. This became my Speed of Cash theory.

It became important for me to buy as many houses as possible so that I could flip them for cash reserves quickly. I knew I needed to increase the number of ways I found deals so that I could build a flipping machine.

It also became more important to me to sell a property quickly – even at a discount – than to wait longer to try to get a higher price. The longer I waited to sell a house, the more I paid in interest and costs, which ate into my profits.

When I started flipping, I would hold out on sales to get the best possible price. But now I was willing to take up to 10 percent less than the full price just to move it – particularly if a house was in a good area, but not a prime area.

I still sold houses at full price. But I learned when to sell at market value and when to discount the price just to move inventory. I also knew that I had to learn new ways to sell properties. I needed to appeal to a wider range of potential buyers.

I read that the No. 1 reason why businesses fail is because they have cash flow problems. If I could keep bringing in profits while maintaining a low overhead, I could avoid this obstacle.

All this would allow me to accumulate cash reserves quickly. Later, by reinvesting the cash, my money would make money faster than I ever could by just working.

Here's an example:

Let's say you make $50,000 a year at your job. This means you are working a minimum of eight hours a day, five days a week and 50 weeks out of the year. This is a total of 2,000 hours to create $50,000.

Now, let's say you are going to flip a house with $50,000 worth of profit. It may take you 20 hours to find that house (which would be a long time in my opinion), one hour to assess the property, six hours to oversee property repairs (you are not doing the construction work) and one hour to close the property (including driving time to title company). This is a total of 28 work hours – less than one week at a regular job!

Now, I can't remember the last time I spent 28 hours flipping a house. In fact, I don't think I have ever spent that many hours flipping a house. However, even if you did, and you calculated your profits at an hourly rate, you would be making $1,785.71 per hour!

Find me a doctor, lawyer or other business professional who would not be happy making that kind of money!

What do you do with the extra time on your hands? Find other deals, work your regular day job or take care of your kids. It doesn't matter, because your cash reserves are building rapidly.

### How Much to Pay

In order to profit from a deal, you have to know how much to pay.

## My $60,000 Mistake

Another one of my mentors was a blind man. Stan learned real estate and made millions as a developer. He was a tough guy.

I had met Stan in California. He owned the house that I rented after the bank foreclosed on my condo. He had also evicted me after one month for not paying rent. Although he was harsh on me, I kept in touch and eventually repaid him.

Later, when I decided to invest in real estate, I called on Stan as a mentor.

In 2002, I consulted Stan about a particular deal. It was a house in a less desirable part of town, but I had bought it extremely under value. A hard-money lender agreed to fund the purchase and repair costs. But the lender would charge a very high 16 percent interest and 3 percent origination fee.

By this time, I had done enough deals that I had about $60,000 cash in the bank. I wanted to use my own money to fund the deal and save on the interest rate that the hard-money lender would charge.

Stan said, "Don't tie up your money in this one deal. Releverage your money." What he meant was that it is better to spend $60,000 on three or four flips than to sink it all into one deal.

"No," I said. "I've got the hang of it now. I can do this."

"OK," he said, "But you have not educated yourself enough to do deals on your own."

I did not take Stan's advice and went on to make the dumbest mistake of my business career. At the time, I thought I knew it all,

The answer is the 70 Percent Rule. This is a formula for how much to pay for any house, in order to make a healthy profit and borrow funds with no money out of pocket. This rule also accounts for repair costs, which can be rolled into the loan so you have fix-up money right off the bat.

The 70 Percent Rule is this: buy any house at 70 percent or less of the fixed-up market value, minus repair costs.

So if you have a house that is worth $100,000 when it is fixed, and the repair costs are $20,000, the maximum you want to pay for it is $50,000.

### The 70 Percent Rule

| | |
|---|---|
| House value after repairs | $100,000 |
| The 70 Percent Rule | x    0.7 |
| | ---------- |
| Subtotal | $ 70,000 |
| Repair costs | - $ 20,000 |
| | ---------- |
| Maximum amount to pay | $ 50,000 |

Can you buy a house for $50,000, or 50 cents on the dollar? Absolutely! When you find motivated sellers and you are able to solve their problems, you can buy houses that fit the 70 Percent Rule all day long.

Let's break it down a bit more. The 70 Percent Rule accounts for 20 percent profit – a healthy margin in the business world – and 10 percent for overhead and holding costs. The repair

just because I had a bit of money in my pocket. Two months later, I lost nearly the entire $60,000.

I had partnered on the deal with a local investor named Craig, who said he had many leads from insurance agents. Craig lacked the years of experience that my mentors had, but he was a smooth talker and seemed trustworthy.

With my strong entrepreneurial spirit and some cash in the bank, I thought I was invincible. I disregarded all the advice my mentors had given: "Work with people who bring more value to your business than you to theirs." "Use other people's money." "Always write a contract."

Stupid as it sounds, I did not write a contract with Craig, sunk more than $57,000 into the project and did not have a system for keeping the contractors accountable.

Halfway through the project, Craig called and said he was opening his own business. He was taking my contacts, contractors and job materials with him, and he wanted half the profits on this deal.

With almost all my capital used up and my contractor gone, I could not finish the job.

Even worse, I later found out that one of the contractors had been overcharging for his work. Craig had approved the invoices and split the excess money with the contractor. Craig had promised to bring more capital to fund the deal; instead, he used my money to pay himself.

And when my money ran out, Craig decided it was time to go out on his own.

I was furious. I was incensed. But I didn't know what to do. I ended up selling the house at a discount, and lost $57,500.

costs will vary according to what a house needs. This amount is subtracted from the 70 percent amount. And the remainder is how much you can pay for the house itself.

If you can negotiate a price less than that amount, even better. That's more money in your pocket. But by using the 70 Percent Rule, you know the maximum you can pay.

The 70 Percent Rule is also the benchmark that most lenders use in the rehab business. So when you use this rule when buying properties, it will be easier to find money as well. When you use the right lenders, you do not have to pay anything out of your own pocket.

### Hard-Money Lenders

Who are the best lenders for rehab properties?
Hard-money lenders.

Hard-money lenders are small companies that specialize in loans for fix-and-flip jobs. They have short-term loans at high interest rates that include repair costs in the loan.

The reason hard-money lenders want to lend you money is because they will earn only 3 to 6 percent interest if they deposit their money in a bank, whereas they make 10 to 18 percent interest on hard-money loans. So it's a good deal for them.

The fact that you are able to buy a house with no money out of pocket, plus have extra for repair costs, makes it a very good deal for you.

That left me with $2,500 in my bank account and many sleepless nights.

I was almost back at ground zero. I was haunted by memories of losing my house, my money, everything again.

I didn't want to tell my mentor. I was so afraid he wouldn't talk to me again. I was so afraid of making more mistakes like this.

Finally, I got the courage to call Stan.

"I told you so," he said, and hung up.

I continued calling him for the next three weeks, leaving messages, begging him to help me – not with money, but with his knowledge, to tell me what to do.

He finally returned my call. "You've shown me that you have the resolve to be successful by constantly leaving me messages on my phone. Now you have to show me that you have the resolve to be successful by educating that stubborn, fat brain of yours.

"Until you prove that you have the humility to be successful, you will do exactly what I say as I say it. And if you ever refuse to listen to me again, I will never mentor you again. I will never answer your phone calls again, no matter how many times you call me."

The man was very harsh, but I knew his words were true.

"I can see you in four days," he said. "Be in my office by noon, or we're done."

Stan knew that I had only $2,500 left, yet he insisted that I spend money on a plane ticket to see him. He wanted me to prove I was truly dedicated. He wanted to see my humility. He was giving me tough love.

Most conventional banks do not want to lend you money for flipping houses. They won't go near a house in need of repairs. They only loan on properties that are in good condition. But there's no profit in houses that are in good condition. Plus, you have to have good credit and usually a hefty down payment to qualify for a bank loan.

Hard-money lenders do not care about your credit or a down payment. They base their loan on the deal itself. Guess what benchmark they use to determine the deal? The 70 Percent Rule. They will lend based on 70 percent of after-repair value, minus repair costs.

Hard money lenders typically do not require a down payment because the equity itself serves as the down payment. When a property price is 70 percent of the after-repair value, the risk is worth the reward. The reward for them is the high interest rate on their money.

At 70 percent, the house has enough equity that if you default on payment, they can easily sell or fix-and-flip the house themselves and make a large profit. This secures the hard-money lender's position and gives them incentive to lend money.

That's why money follows deals. If you can find a great deal, money always follows.

### Private Investors

Private investors are wealthy individuals who do not lend money professionally. These are people with 401(k)s, IRAs,

So I flew out. And he taught me what I needed to know.

That mistake was a $60,000 lesson. It was the most expensive training seminar in my life. The stupid thing was that if I had just listened to Stan, I could have turned that $60,000 into $100,000, rather than a $60,000 loss.

This is why I now preach: Enthusiasm is great, but enthusiasm headed in the wrong direction is certain failure. Not until I listened to my mentor did I point my enthusiasm and education in the right direction for success.

As for the house, Stan taught me several ways to ensure that a contractor never takes advantage and overcharges. He also taught me how to enter a business deal with safety nets so that I would never lose my savings again.

Stan's mentorship paid off many times over.

SEP plans, lines of credit, equity in their homes, or just plain cash. Such individuals are all potential private investors. The enticement for a private investor is the rate of return on their investment. In contrast, the motivation for a hard-money lender is the deal, or the ability to lend their money against a secure investment.

Most private investors will lend at a 10 percent to 16 percent return. But you can sometimes negotiate the interest rate to as little as 8 percent. For private investors, the return they make on rehab loans beats what the bank will pay. And it is secured by a lien on the house. So it's a good deal for them.

If you offer healthy returns on their investment, you will always find people to lend you money on your rehab projects.

### Partners

Business partners are great. I have used many types of partners on deals for different reasons. I have partnered with a wholesaler, the homeowner who was selling me the house, a friend, businesspeople with a little money to put down and so on.

Let's say you don't have good credit and your lender wants you to have good credit. Wouldn't it be worth finding a credit partner to split the profits, rather than make no money? The same goes for a cash partner, for the same reason.

You want to take on partners on a deal-by-deal basis only. Take partners who bring money or credit and can help you acquire properties.

# Chapter 11

## Learning to Sell
### *Creating Excited Buyers and Sellers*

- **Selling by Auction**
- **Owner-Financed Deals**
- **No Junk Fees**
- **Expanding My Team**
- **Following My Instincts**

### Selling by Auction

One day, Veronica and I went to a home and garden show. I had no intention of buying anything, but she wanted new furniture.

I made it very clear that I did not want to buy new furniture for our new house. I thought the furniture we had would work just fine. But Veronica – being the savvy saleswoman she is – took me to where they were holding a furniture auction.

Before I knew it, I was caught up in the frenzy. I raised my hand to bid, and I was hooked. At the end, I walked out with thousands of dollars of furniture that I had had no intention of buying.

The items up for bid opened at half their retail price. However, I let my competitive spirit get the best of me and I got caught up in the buying frenzy. After several winning bids, I walked out feeling

However, the most important thing to understand is that you don't need a business partner. Again, if you have a great deal, you will have a wide range of choices for funding it. With each deal, figure what works best for you and do that.

### Funding Systems

When you set up your business systems, you want to include documents for funding deals, so you can get it done quickly and easily.

In my Flip and Grow Rich program, I have more than 12 packages of documents for funding deals, including:

- Financing Approval Letters to Sellers
- Private Investor Agreements
- Lender Applications
- Closing Loans Checklist

You want to have these systems in place so that you can move quickly and focus on activities that generate income.

like I had gotten some great deals. But I still paid more than I had expected, because I never planned to buy anything in the first place.

Then I had a money-making moment. I realized I could start selling my houses by auction.

At first, nobody showed up at my house auctions. I realized that starting bids at full price didn't work. I kept tweaking it. I found that when I started bids at half price – just like at the furniture auction – I got lots of bids. Instead of having a speaking auction, I also turned it into a silent auction. Instead of a two-hour bidding window, I gave it the full weekend. This helped push the prices higher. People who got the houses were thrilled because they had beaten out so many people to buy it.

Now my houses up for auction sold in a weekend. This helped move inventory and turn equity into profits much more quickly.

I also found new ways to market my houses. I posted banners and signs and handed out fliers throughout the neighborhood.

People in the neighborhoods where we sold houses were usually very supportive. Many were happy that we could take a beat-up house – often an eyesore – and turn it into something beautiful. They were grateful because their house values went up, too.

## Owner-Financed Deals

Another selling technique I learned was owner financing.

I attended a real estate seminar in 2003, where I heard a speaker talk about selling properties through real estate agents, which was pretty basic.

# Chapter K

## Ways to Sell
Realize Profits with an Array of Options

- **Plan Your Exits**
- **Wider Range of Buyers**
- **Strategies for Cash Flow**
- **Real Estate Agents**
- **Auctions**
- **Owner Financing**
- **Lease Options**
- **Wholesaling**
- **Selling to Landlords**
- **Selling Systems**
- **Marketing Systems**

### Plan Your Exits

The fact is that you make your money when you buy. But you get paid when you sell. As soon as you are thinking about buying a property, you want to start thinking about how you are going to sell it.

Although I buy a lot of properties, I am a very safe investor. One way I do that is to think about how I can sell my

The investor sitting next to me seemed to think the same. "I have a much better way," he said. "None of those guys up there know what I know."

That piqued my curiosity. "What do you do?" I said.

"I do owner financing," he said. "I just take the note, and I sell it to other banks." He explained that this worked well for houses in lower-income neighborhoods, where buyers often did not qualify for conventional bank loans.

After that, I learned everything I could about owner financing. Selling houses through owner financing became a big way for me to do business and make money. For about three years, I sold nearly 60 percent of my houses through owner financing.

In more recent years, I've been selling about 30 percent of houses this way, only because I have more upscale houses in my inventory. Upscale houses tend to attract more people who can qualify for conventional bank loans, so they do not need owner financing.

**No Junk Fees**

As the business grew, I started accumulating inventory. Most growing businesses experience cash flow problems. I wanted to prevent this up front. I knew that in order to keep cash coming, houses had to sell.

One challenge is that some mortgage brokers charge ridiculous origination fees, tack on too many loan points or add all kinds of "junk" fees. Unfortunately, I met many lackadaisical mortgage brokers who got loans done on their sweet time, not on my time frame.

With these mortgage brokers, my potential buyers would end up

properties quickly. The market – whether it is hot, cold or flat – does not dictate if a property is going to sell. The market simply determines how I'm going to sell the house.

Most people have been taught only one way to sell a house: through real estate agents. They are great. But you want to make sure you also have other ways to sell.

When you go into a property, think about at least three ways to sell it. Never approach an investment with only one way to sell it. Always think about multiple exit strategies, multiple ways to make money.

This will help keep your financial juices flowing. It also helps you sleep well at night. To be an educated investor is to be a creative investor. The more educated you get and the more creative you become, the faster you will move your properties and put money in your pocket.

Some selling strategies you can use are real estate agents, auctions, lease options, owner finance, wholesaling and selling to landlords. You can use different strategies depending on what you want to achieve in any given market.

**Wider Range of Buyers**

By having different exit strategies, you can sell to a wider range of buyers.

If you have a property that has appreciated quickly, you can use a real estate agent to find buyers who qualify for conventional loans.

walking away because the extra $2,000 in loan fees would put them over the edge. Or they would start shopping mortgage brokers, so the closings would be delayed. Instead of closing in 30 days, the houses would close in 45 days or more.

I realized that I needed a good mortgage broker on my team. I found someone who wasn't a mortgage broker but worked for a mortgage broker. He was ambitious but didn't know too much about the industry.

"I'm going to make a deal with you," I said. "You're going to charge a flat two points for every deal. That's 2 percent of the loan amount."

That mortgage guy got so much business from me that he opened his own mortgage broker firm. I took him from being an employee to a business owner. Now he runs his own mortgage broking company. He solved many of my problems, and I solved many of his financial problems.

My mortgage broker helped me in another big way. When his grandfather died, the family had an estate sale. They sold the house to me at a big discount. I moved out of my small rented office and turned that house into my office.

**Expanding My Team**

I expanded my team in other ways.

One attorney I worked with gave me a steady supply of leads. He had clients with problems. One group of clients he worked with owned townhouses that were flooded and they were suing the developer. He called me and I bought the townhouses. Later, I hired him as my own attorney.

I also hired a project manager. By now, I had worked out invoicing

If you meet a buyer who has a good down payment but bad credit, you can sell by owner finance. If someone has good credit but no down payment, you can steer them toward a mortgage broker and sell through a real estate agent.

If you have a property in a slow or flat market, you can sell it to a landlord. In such markets, rents tend to go up, which give landlords a positive cash flow.

### Strategies for Cash Flow

You can also use different exit strategies to achieve various cash flow goals.

If you sell through a real estate agent to a buyer with a conventional loan, you can generate cash now. You can also sell by auction and take profits now. If you sell using owner finance, you can get some cash now and more later when you sell the note in six months to a year. If you do a lease option, you can get some cash now, monthly cash flow and the balance when the tenant buys in one to two years. Another way to make cash now is to take smaller profits by wholesaling the unrepaired house to another rehabber. You can also make money by selling to a landlord.

All these strategies will give you short, medium and long-term cash or cash flow, depending on which you use.

If you are just starting your flipping career, the ideal scenario is to get cash now. But having several strategies gives you different fall-back plans in case any one does not work out.

and management systems with my contractors. I also figured out how to use my computer to manage projects.

By the time I was flipping more than 20 houses per month, I was ready to take on a project manager to oversee these systems. My project manager used the computer and fax machine. He did not need to use his car and check on properties all the time.

All this freed up my time to focus on what I do best: finding and making deals.

## Following My Instincts

As my business grew, I developed new ways to buying, funding and selling houses. This was how I created a "flipping machine."

I eventually developed more than eight ways to find properties. I also had more than six ways to sell any given property. I used different selling strategies, depending on the market or what I wanted to achieve. I sold by auction when I wanted to entertain myself. I used a realtor when the market values were high. Or I would use lease options or owner financing when I needed to move a property quickly.

I did not rely on any single strategy. But having different types of exit strategies gave me a lot more options. When I walked into a house, I would have several different exits in mind before I even bought it.

Over time, I discovered new ways of buying, funding and selling houses. Some people said there was nothing else to be taught in real estate, but that was not true for me. First I was a student of the game, then a master of my sport. I was always finding new ways to do things. I did it because it's fun, exciting and challenging.

That's what I call being a safe investor. Whether you flip two houses a year or 20 a month, you can be safe and smart by having at least three exit strategies for each house.

This is not just about increasing the quantity of money in your pocket. It's about increasing your quality of life. When you close your eyes at night, you want to be able to sleep peacefully. Just knowing that you can get out of a property at any time using different selling strategies will help you sleep well. That way, your quality of life does not have to go down while your income goes up.

## Selling Strategies for Cash Flow

| Goal: | Cash now | Medium-term Cash or Cash flow | Long-term Cash or Cash flow |
|---|---|---|---|
| | 1 week – 2 months | 2 months – 2 years | 2 or more years |
| Selling Strategy: | | | |
| Real Estate Agent | X | | |
| Auction | X | | |
| Owner Finance | X | X | X |
| Lease Option | X | X | X |
| Wholesale | X | | |
| Landlords | X | | |

With experience, I combined my real world savvy with the advice and strategies of my mentors. If you're on a deserted island, you might be a professional, but you have no survival skills. That is why I was so successful so quickly; I chose not to make myself a desert island. I followed my mentors to success and you should too. The funny thing about desert islands is they are vacant for a reason: you cannot thrive on them.

However, before I created a system, I was a slave to my own ignorance.

## Real Estate Agents

Real estate agents can be a great re

However, if you use an agent, find a good on
my opinion means someone who sells at least $1 m
properties a year. You want an agent with a good marketing
plan for your property. Anybody can list a house on the
multiple-listing service. But selling the house requires an active
marketing plan.

You want to find out: Is the agent a good communicator? Does
the agent plan to hold open houses? Will he or she send notices
to all the brokerage offices within a three-mile radius of the
property? Put these agreements in your listing contract.

Do not become dependent on real estate agents to sell your
property. Make sure you have multiple ways to exit a property –
to keep your cash flow going and build your cash reserves.

You must also know what type of market you're selling in. Is it a
better market for real estate agents? Or is it a better market for
other types of sales strategies?

If it's a hot market, real estate agents are great. If you are
targeting middle and upper income buyers, real estate agents
can help you sell. For slower markets and lower-income buyers,
I prefer to sell by owner financing.

You can also combine strategies, as long as you have agreements
in place with your agent. You can tell them that if you find
an owner-finance buyer before the agent finds a conventional
buyer, you will pay them a small fee, but not a commission.

# pter 12

## Finding Balance
*Remembering My "Why"*

- **Late Dinner Talks**
- **What Veronica Needed**
- **Flipping from Happiness**

## Late Dinner Talks

Veronica and I had an agreement. While Mondo Man was still a baby, her job was to take care of him. My job was to provide for our family.

When Mondo Man was 3 1/2 years old, in 2002, we took him to a private school. We walked him to the playground, led him into the school and said goodbye. Then we walked out and got in the car. He came bolting out of the school, ran through two heavy metal doors and stood in the parking lot. We realized he wasn't ready for school yet, so we decided to let Veronica continue taking care of him until he was older.

By summer 2002, I was working seven days a week, flipping three to four houses at a time. I was hardly ever home. I would start at 6 a.m. and get back to the house around 11 p.m. By this time, Veronica was 26 and I was 32. I didn't realize it at the time, but I was starting to lose sight of the reason for working so hard: my family.

Real estate agents can be effective in a slow market if you are listing a house under value and the house is in good condition. But you need to make sure they are highly experienced, with a great sales strategy behind them.

## Auctions

If you want to sell a property fast, you can use the auction strategy early in the game, before listing it with a real estate agent. Your goal here is to sell to someone with a conventional loan.

The key to a successful auction is to create a competitive environment that does not seem competitive. The auctions that most people know about are verbal auctions. The auctions I do are silent auctions.

Selling by auction creates a buying frenzy. When selling by auction, start the bid price at half the market value. When the price gets as close as possible to the price you want, the house goes to the highest bidder.

If you do not reach your reserve amount – the price you wanted on the house – you do not have to award it to anybody. You can outbid everybody and sell it to yourself. You are not legally bound to accept these offers, because no one met your reserve price.

At that point, you can use another selling strategy, such as turning the house over to a real estate agent for conventional listing and sales.

Earlier that year, we had moved out of the two-bedroom apartment and into a 3,000-square-foot house that I had bought on an owner-finance basis. My credit was still too low to qualify for a good loan, so I bought the house from someone who held the underlying mortgage in his name.

Veronica was a great wife and mother. She took care of the house and cooked great dinners. But I was never home to enjoy them.

"I'll have dinner ready for you," Veronica would say. But I would still be managing contractors.

"Mondo Man and I are going to eat dinner first," she would say. But I would still have to meet a seller.

Then, it was "Mondo Man and I are going to bed first." But I would still be faxing appraisal orders. When I finally came home, I would heat up dinner and eat alone.

More and more, when the three of us were together, Mondo Man would go to his mommy. He wouldn't come to me. He knew who I was, but we weren't as close as I would have liked.

One night, Veronica came down from the bedroom and sat down next to me while I ate dinner. It was about 11 p.m. "You know what?" she asked.

"Uh-oh," I thought. "It's one of those talks again."

"What?" I asked.

Veronica continued: "We only have one child. We aren't going to have anymore children. We only have one opportunity to do it right. We can't screw it up."

### Owner Financing

Owner financing is another way to move inventory quickly. These deals are useful for selling homes to people who may not qualify for conventional bank loans. They have bad credit, but have money for a down payment.

With owner financing, you basically became the bank. You can finance the entire loan for the buyer and sell the note to a note buyer. This is another way to make quick cash.

You disclose to the buyer that you have an underlying mortgage and create a new mortgage for them. You take a down payment and charge an interest rate on the monthly payment, just like a bank.

Then you sell that note to a note buyer at a discount and take profit. When banks such as Wells Fargo or Bank of America hold a mortgage, they sell the mortgage – also called a note – to other banks. They don't ask the homeowner permission to sell the note, they just do it.

### Lease Options

Lease options are useful when you want to sell a house quickly. They are useful if payments are coming due on a property and you have to generate income quickly.

Lease option deals tend to go quickly. They generate money for you in three ways:

• the up-front option payment that the tenant pays

I continued to eat my enchilada.

"He's little right now," Veronica continued. "But before you know it, he's going to be 8, then 12, then 16, then 20. And you'll say he grew up so fast. You never knew him."

She was right. I didn't like what she said, but it resonated with me. "Yeah," I said.

So I started coming home early for dinner. I'd be back by 7 p.m. But even then, my mind was racing. One night, Veronica let me know.

She was talking about something, but I wasn't really paying attention.

"Hmm, babe?" I asked.

Veronica took a deep breath. "You're here, but you're not present to talk to me," she said. "It's nice to have a warm body here, but you're always thinking."

"I'm sorry, babe," I said. "But I can't help it. I've got to get this deal done. You know I need to provide for my family."

"Fine, you're providing for us," she said. "But that's not what makes a family."

I just sat with my mouth shut.

"You still have me and Mondo Man," she said. "You're still his father. You're still the leader of the family. But right now, you're married to your business. You need to do maybe one or two flips a month. You need to find some balance in your life."

I realized that working fewer hours wasn't the answer, because my mind was still racing. But I was swamped with deals, and I wasn't going to give it up. I was driven to succeed.

- the cash flow on the monthly payment

- and profit from the sale, when the tenant actually buys the house

A lease option is when a tenant rents a house with the option of buying it within a certain amount of time, usually one to two years. This gives them enough time to clean up their credit to qualify for a regular bank mortgage. Or they might be going through a divorce, so they do not want to own property yet. A lease option is a great way to meet the needs of people who want to make a commitment to a property but are not yet ready to own.

So, if it's a $200,000 house, they might put down $10,000 in option money as a deposit. Then they lease it for, say, $2,000 a month. Maybe you will make $300 in cash flow on the monthly payment. And when they finally close, you can make a profit on the equity for, say, $50,000. This equity is the difference between what you owe on the house and what you are selling it for, less the $10,000 option payment.

The other benefit to lease options is that the tenant-buyer is usually more committed and more responsible. Tenant-buyers tend to take better care of a house because they want to eventually buy it. They think of it as their own home.

### Wholesaling

If you want some fast cash, you can sell your deal on a wholesale basis to another investor. Other rehabbers – not potential homeowners – are your target sales market.

## What Veronica Needed

One day, Veronica brought me lunch at the office. It was late 2002. I was managing contractors, workers and the office. It was nuts.

Veronica and Mondo Man sat down in chairs on the other side of my desk. She pulled out sandwiches from a bag and spread them out.

I closed the door and sat at my desk.

Veronica started talking about what we were going to do that weekend, where we were going to go. Mondo Man squirmed around in his seat.

As Veronica talked, the phone rang. I took the call.

When I hung up, Veronica started talking again.

Then, one of the contractors knocked on the door and came in. He wanted to know what color to paint the outside of a flip. I told him.

When I finished, another contractor walked in. People were coming and going, needing this, asking that.

Veronica furrowed her brow and pursed her lips. She and Mondo Man had almost finished their sandwiches, but I had only taken one bite out of mine.

Veronica looked at me straight in the eyes and said, "I want at least 30 minutes of your time."

I shut my phone off. I told the guys to stay out of the office. I could feel her tension.

You will typically do a "double close" when selling by wholesale. That means you will close with your seller on the same day that you close with the rehab buyer. This saves you from bringing money to the table, getting a loan and paying extra fees.

If you do this, make sure you educate yourself as to exactly how to do this, to avoid sellers and buyers going around you and cutting you out of the deal.

### Selling to Landlords

Landlords will buy in hot or cold markets. If you offer a good deal, they can also become potential buyers in any market.

But a cold market is a particularly good time to remember landlords, because when markets go down, rents go up. It's simple supply and demand.

When markets go down, lenders become much stricter because properties are not holding their values as well. So when markets go down, people lose their jobs. If people are losing jobs, mortgage companies are not writing bank loans as easily, and foreclosures go up. When foreclosures go up, fewer people own homes, so guess what they do? Rent.

Now the demand for rental houses goes up. Then supply goes down, which pushes rents higher. When rents go up, they create a positive cash flow because property values have gone down.

Houses that used to be too expensive for landlords are now affordable, because rents have gone up. They are making

When we were alone, she finally said slowly but deliberately: "I am a woman. I need attention."

"What do you mean you need attention?" I raised my voice. "I'm here!"

"Let me tell you what," she said. "The reason I think people get divorced is that they work really hard. And the woman starts to look for someone else. Or if the woman doesn't find someone else, the man will go and find another woman. It's not the sex they want. It's because they need attention. And I need attention."

I got really angry. "Are you telling me you want to leave? Are you telling me you don't want to be with me?"

She said, "I have no intentions on anyone else, I have no desire for anyone else, I don't want to be with anyone else. You're the man I want. You're the man I married. You're the man of my dreams. But I want your attention. And if not, we're going to grow further and further apart, and someone's going to go looking for attention – either me or you. And we're not going to be together. That's how it works."

She continued: "Most women don't tell their husbands these things until it's too late. They tell them in all different ways they need attention, but they don't flat out tell them. Then they go out and look for it. I need attention. Otherwise, our marriage will break up, because women need attention from men."

I was upset, but I knew enough to keep listening.

Veronica said: "Do you know when women need attention?"

"When?"

"All the time," she said.

positive cash flow. And because you're buying at 30 cents on the dollar instead of 70 cents on the dollar in a hot market, your profit margin is wider. The landlord also benefits from the spread because it gives him more cash flow.

If you want to sell the house to a landlord even more quickly, put in a good tenant with a strong lease application and rental agreement.

### Selling Systems

Paperwork is an important part of your business systems. It enables you to sell your properties quickly and put cash in your pocket as soon as possible.

My Flip and Grow Rich system includes paperwork for selling properties eight different ways. These include selling by:

- auctions
- lease options
- owner finance
- and more

### Marketing Systems

You also want to have marketing systems in your business to help you reach potential buyers.

In my Flip and Grow Rich system, I have sample paperwork and scripts to do marketing through:

"OK."

I was still angry but I knew she had a point.

I sat back and fumed. After about an hour, I thought that it was smart of her to be honest and lay all the cards on the table. I knew she told me these things because she loved me.

## Flipping from Happiness

I started taking every other weekend off. It felt really strange at first. Then I'd get behind on work. I was coming home for dinner at 7 p.m., but I would still be on the phone. I attempted to work less. But my business was still growing and thriving. By now it was 2003, and I was still chained to my business.

But Veronica is not one to give up. One night, we had another talk.

"We need you here," she said. "You are our leader and we need you."

I thought, "Why is this so hard? Why am I still struggling so much? Why is this still not working?"

Veronica continued. "Why are you doing this?"

I hardened my expression and said: "You have to understand, after you came out of the hospital, it was equally hard for me. We were living in your dad's garage; I lost your dad's loan. Then I had to borrow money from my dad. Now that I'm making money, I want to impress them that I'm a winner. I'm not the guy who was on unemployment."

Veronica's voiced softened. "You don't need to impress anybody," she said. "The only people in the world you need to impress are me and Mondo Man."

- ads
- signs
- fliers
- voicemail
- and more

By having systems, you can execute any strategy with ease. By having several exit strategies, you can generate cash now, create cash flow for the medium term or build wealth for the long term.

You can start now.

Contact my team at 1-800-771-6202 x 4001.

That's when it hit me. I was living a rich life, but I still had a poor mentality. I was so afraid of living in a garage and I was still trying to get away from being poor. I knew that if that's what I was focused on, that's what I would ultimately get. That's called making money out of fear. That was not making money out of happiness.

After Veronica said that, I just took a deep breath. I could finally give myself permission to enjoy our life together. I could give myself permission to make money out of happiness, not fear.

Veronica was right. My family is important to me, and somehow I had gotten away from that. I realized that I needed to continue flipping, because I was hugely passionate about it. And I wanted to set it up so that I could spend time with my family.

We had gotten through the hardest part of our lives, and I did not want to lose our family now.

I realized that people have an ability to survive really tough times. But when it's over, we take it easy, and everything else does not seem so bad. Then things can slowly deteriorate, because it's still better than not having food on the table or being homeless – or in my case, nearly losing my wife and son at the hospital.

I was working really hard to feed my family because it was better than being broke. I had raised my standards financially, but I lowered my expectations for my family life. I could have easily taken my family for granted, simply because they were around.

I was working so hard because I wanted my family to have a better life and I wanted to create a family legacy. I wanted my son to think his father was a winner, to be proud of me. But what would it mean if one day I passed my legacy on to my son, yet he didn't know who I was? Nothing.

# Chapter L

**True Wealth**
Remember Your "Why"

- **Definition of Wealth**
- **Create Balance**
- **Clean Your Garage**
- **Schedule Activities**
- **Part-Time Investing**

**Definition of Wealth**

You can get very, very rich flipping houses. You can spend all your time working and getting rich. But you won't be wealthy.

Wealth comes from having balance in your life. This is my definition of wealth:

"Wealth is the infinite belief that you can provide an abundance of money, you can create an abundance of money, or tap into an abundance of money – at anytime."

After that, I loved Veronica even more. I saw how she had a great way of talking to me about things before problems arose. She was able to see the signs and let me know before issues got too big.

I appreciated that she was so open and honest about her feelings with me. That created a very fun, dynamic and interesting relationship. It was extremely positive for us.

Veronica was right. I needed to create balance between work and my family life. I just needed to figure out how.

## Create Balance

If you work all the time and do not give something back to yourself, you may grow rich, but you won't necessarily be happy. Finding time for activities that do not generate income but that you enjoy can help you create a greater sense of peace.

While you're busy making money, remember the needs of your loved ones. Flipping houses is not about working so much that you don't have time for them. Leave a legacy for your loved ones, but don't forget about them along the way.

## Clean Your Garage

You can't make a great living with a filthy garage. It's tough to make a lot of money when your life is in shambles.

It's a funny thing, but the majority of people I have met whose houses go into foreclosure have garages that are a wreck. There's stuff everywhere.

The majority of people I know who are millionaires have garages that are totally in order. They might have a barbecue going in the backyard, get a football out of the garage and everything is in perfect working order.

Some people may say that's not a fair scenario, but the garage is a metaphor for life: the more your personal life is in order the easier it is to make money, because you don't have other things weighing on your mind. That is the essence of finding balance.

How do you find balance in your life?

# Chapter 13

## Building Systems
### *Work Less and Earn More*

- **Ideal Scenario**
- **The Employee Mistake**
- **Duplicating Myself**
- **Challenges**
- **Systems**
- **Less Time, More Money**

## Ideal Scenario

I was motivated to find a balance between my work and family life. It was important to me to be successful, but also to have my family with me to enjoy it.

I realized that I needed to find a way to replace myself in the business instead of doing everything myself. I needed systems.

When I looked at my mastermind group on my office wall, I focused on Bill Gates. I thought that he must be an amazing systems person. He must be really organized. He inspired me to create my own business system.

I wanted a scenario where the business didn't consume my thoughts. When I came home, I wanted to be able to concentrate on my family,

Take care of your health. If you're married, spend time with your spouse. If you have kids, spend time with them and create magical moments that they'll remember.

If you're not married, spend time with your significant other, friends or family. Do physical activities that keep you away from the television and out of the house. The point is to do things that create joy in your life.

## Schedule Activities

The average millionaire schedules vacations one year in advance.

If you schedule things that are important to you far in advance, you will keep balance. In your daily life, schedule your work and family time. Then, keep those commitments.

Whether you are single, married or have kids, explain to your loved ones that your work time is for work, not play. When you have family time, focus on your family. Do not answer phone calls and pay bills. If you're a single parent, scheduling your time is even more important.

You can also streamline your schedule. Do you see activities in your schedule that are not productive? Cut them out. Do you have too much drinking time? Cut that out. Do you have activities that are not productive or can be done by someone else? Change it or delegate it. You want to focus on productive activities, which is making money or spending time with loved ones.

You must realize that in order to be successful, you must develop good habits. Start building good habits now, instead of

not my business. I asked myself: "How can I take my mind out of this scenario? When I walk away, how can I shut off the cell phone and computer? How can I shut everything off more often?"

This was around late 2002 and early 2003. My business was growing and I was generating more income. I was on track for my biggest year ever.

## The Employee Mistake

That was when I made another big mistake: hiring employees. It was a nightmare.

In 2002, I had a small office and lean staff. The office was a one-room, 350-square-foot space. Rent was $500. It had three desks – one for me, one for a guy who helped me find properties and one for a secretary.

But I wanted to expand the business on a massive scale. And I wanted the office and staff to support it. By 2003, I had moved the office to a huge, 2,500-square-foot warehouse, and I hired 26 employees to help me fix up properties: carpenters, painters, tile setters, trim laborers and others.

I hired employees because I thought it could cut costs. I figured that I could reduce my expenses by half by having my own full-time crew instead of hiring contractors.

But it didn't turn out that way. I thought that if I had a paint bill for $8,000 on a house, I could cut it to $4,000. But it actually cost me $10,000.

That's because if you pay a paint contractor by the job, he's going to work as quickly as he possibly can so he can move on to the next job. But if you pay an employee $15 an hour to paint, he does not

waiting till "some day," which might never come.

These habits include scheduling activities that make your life complete and add to your sense of satisfaction. Wealth is the satisfaction that you are truly doing what you want to with your life.

## Part-Time Investing

With my system, you do not need a lot more extra time to flip houses. But you need to control your time. You can check deals on your computer during your lunch breaks. If you have small children, organize your time so that you work after putting them to bed.

You can always find deals with your computer, check out the property values and later have your contractors go to the property itself. With my system, you only need check on your project two to four times during the entire flip – when you buy it, when you rehab it and when you sell it. You will spend maybe a maximum of 15 hours with a house. That's great pay.

With this system, you don't need to get on your hands and knees and do the work yourself. You simply do the deal and manage the project.

That's why real estate investing can be a part-time job. As long as you schedule your time, you can make money investing while spending time doing other things you love to do.

care how long it takes because he's going to get paid $15 an hour, anyway. There was a laziness factor. There was little motivation to get things done.

It also was a nightmare to manage so many people. Sometimes they would show up, sometimes they would not. One guy might get paid more than the other guy, so the other guy wants to get paid the same. Then there are all these legalities. You have to pay federal employee taxes, social security and Medicare.

There's a difference between being an entrepreneur and being a manager. I was being a manager of people. I wasn't spending as much time going out and looking for deals. I was still buying a ton of properties, but because jobs were getting done more slowly, properties weren't moving as quickly. That was costing me money.

It took me about six months to actually look at the books and figure it out. I realized that I was still making money, but I wasn't maximizing profits.

So I let people go. I did it over a period of six months, and I gave people two months to find new jobs so they could feed their families. Or I hired them back as subcontractors. When I turned people into subcontractors, their productivity picked up and so did profits. Now, rather than taking eight weeks to get a house done using employees, it would take four weeks with subcontractors.

After this experience, I decided not to run an employee-based business again. I focused on using subcontractors.

I also wanted a system for managing contractors so that I could spend less time working in the business.

# Chapter M

## How to Fix
Use Systems to Streamline Construction

- **Fix Houses for Maximum Profit**
- **Cookie-Cutter Rules**
- **Seven Rules to Maximize Profits**
- **Assessing Repairs**
- **Dealing with Animal Odors**
- **Replace Yourself**
- **Paperwork Systems**
- **How to Manage Contractors**
- **Contractor Paperwork**

### Fix Houses for Maximum Profit

Finding a house is where you make your profit. Funding is where you get your money. Fixing is where you keep your money.

The key to fixing a house is speed, speed, speed. You don't want to be involved in the activity of fixing up the house. You want to have a system so that you can control the project to stay on time and within budget.

## Duplicating Myself

Around this time, my brother-in-law introduced me to a very successful guy in multilevel marketing. He sold various products.

He told me something very interesting. He said that the top multilevel marketers are successful because they are able to duplicate themselves. They line up a lot of people to work downstream from them and do exactly what they do.

I thought, "What if I could duplicate myself in my own business? It's difficult to find someone who would work as hard or be just as determined as myself.

"Well, what if I could have other people do parts of my business? What if I could have other people do parts of my system and I didn't have to make them employees? What if the work could get done the way I wanted without me being there?"

I needed to create a system to do this.

I realized that there are lenders, real estate agents, title companies, insurance companies – all there to help me. And they were all getting paid on commission. Why have them work for me like employees? Make a system. Have them talk to each other.

That way they didn't have to call me about every other thing and then I would have to call the next guy about every other thing. They could just call each other directly and get it done.

So I began to develop a system. It took about eight months of trying different ideas and ironing out kinks before I had a system that really took off.

In my system, we use the exact same product models and colors in every house, including: ceiling fans, kitchen cabinets, countertops, tile, walls, ceilings, and carpet.

Are there variations to that? Of course. You will need to use your common sense.

In the TV show, we highlight the most challenging flips, because they have the most opportunities for viewers to learn. But in my flipping business, I use a cookie-cutter system, with cookie-cutter formulas to turn out houses on a day-to-day basis. As you build your flipping business, that's also what you want to do.

### Cookie-Cutter Rules

When you are fixing a house, you want to streamline your repair activity in order to maximize profits. If you go over budget or take too long to finish your house, you may make money, but not as much as you could.

Remember, just because you are making money does not mean you are maximizing profits. You want to keep your costs lean to maximize profits.

### Seven Rules to Maximize Profits

1. Do not overdo it on flips. Most times, reaching a nine out of 10 on a house is good enough. Most buyers want to customize the look to their own tastes. They would rather buy a blank canvas.

## Challenges

By now, I had three areas of challenge: contractors, paperwork and project management.

My contractors were driving me nuts. They asked me questions at all times of the day, every day of the week. Questions like: "Where are the materials?" "How do I do this job?" "When do I do that job?" or "When do I get paid?" Or I would pay them and they would take Fridays off. Sometimes they would finish a job, but it still had this missing or that not done right, so I would have to walk through the house multiple times before all the work was done to satisfaction. Sometimes after doing several jobs with me, the contractors would get too comfortable, and I would have to fire them.

I needed to create a system for managing contractors.

Paperwork was also a challenge. At this stage, my inventory was a roller-coaster ride. I might flip eight houses in one month, then two houses the next. The paperwork for all these deals was eating my time – sending offers to sellers, ordering title, signing contracts, requesting draws from lenders. I spent half my time with the fax machine.

I was still making money, but managing all these things was slowing me down.

I needed a project manager. I had gotten really good at assessing repairs. I could pop my head into a house, look around and know how much everything would cost to rehab. But with as many deals as I had, I didn't have time to do that anymore. Yet I wasn't quite sure how to replace myself.

Earlier, I had hired two project managers. Each was in charge of different houses. But soon they were coming to me with problems rather than

2. Do not remodel the house. If you rip out walls, put in new archways or add doorways to a house, it will eat your profits. Leaving it alone is usually good enough.

3. Do not use colored paint. Most buyers like a neutral color, and they may paint over the colors you choose. Leave it plain.

4. Do not use extra trim or fancy fixtures. That may feed your ego, but buyers do not always want them. And these extras eat your profits. Unless the house has serious design flaws, leave the walls alone.

5. Do not become a charity. Manage your contractors to get the job done on time and within budget. Give contractors strict deadlines. You can even have penalty fees for not completing work on time. If a house takes too long to finish, you will be giving away your money.

6. Do not become an employer. Hire contractors, but do not turn them into employees. When flipping houses, an army of entrepreneurs is more efficient than a cast of employees.

7. You are an investor. You look at returns, not decorating ideas. Focus on profits, not activity.

## Assessing Repairs

Every time I walk into a house, I have a checklist of repairs. I have a system that lists what needs to be done and how much it will cost. It makes it very easy for me to manage each project.

When you assess repairs, you will want to look at what is needed outside and inside the house.

solving my problems for me. I realized they had too much time on their hands. It wasn't lifting my load, it was adding to it.

I knew I needed a system for project management. It did not mean hiring more people. It meant having better systems.

## Systems

I created several systems for handling these challenges.

First, I came up with a system for invoicing my contractors. They could only invoice me on certain days of the week before 5 p.m. They had to give me pictures of the properties. They would get paid only on certain days. They had contractual penalties for missing deadlines. They had to follow the system, or they got fired.

I made shopping lists for my contractors. Every house now had the same color paint, bathroom tile, light fixtures and kitchen cabinets. Every product had a model number, color and price. My contractors knew exactly what to do and what to buy. It took the guesswork out of everything.

I also invented a paperwork system. I would send the same order sheet to my money lender, appraiser, title company processor, insurance agent and contractors. They now all had the same information – address, lockbox code, repair costs, etc. – so they didn't have to keep calling me with questions. They also had one another's contact information so they could talk to each other – not just to me – to get things done.

I organized my papers into a filing system that easily tracked everything. I had a way to file rejected offers, so that I could resubmit bids in 30 days. If the offers were accepted, I could move forward quickly.

Areas to assess outside the house:

- foundations
- roofs
- soffits and fascias
- siding
- landscaping

Areas to assess inside the house:

- walls
- ceilings
- paint
- floors
- kitchen
- electrical boxes
- light fixtures
- master bedroom
- bathrooms
- water heater
- plumbing
- doors
- doorknobs

In my system, the checklist for each house becomes part of the overall project management. That way, I reduce the number of trips I need to take. And it maximizes my profits.

I turned my computer into a project manager. Invoices, photos, finance approval letters, offers and market research – everything was now done through e-mail, the Internet and data files.

My title company became an extension of my business. The processors there handled my contracts, prepared title and did all kinds of other work.

Years later, when I had the TV show, we would rehab houses using different colors and tailor-made features. But these are only a small percentage of the houses I do. For the vast majority of houses I flip in the business, I use standard product lists.

I became addicted to making systems. I hunkered down for a whole week just creating systems. The business took a dip, but it was worth it.

As I developed these systems, I became less of a slave to my business. I could spend more time looking for deals, not just managing them. I could focus on making money, not just being busy. I was no longer a manager. I was an investor.

## Less Time, More Money

Something amazing then happened. My business shifted. I was no longer an employee in my business. I was now the business owner. I was spending less time in my business, but my business kept growing.

It was fantastic. I didn't have to always be there, thinking about the business, handling problems. I didn't work harder anymore. I worked smarter. The business was no longer running me. I was running the business.

The less time I spent with the business, the more time I had for my family. I could pick up my son from school. We would spend

**Dealing with Animal Odors**

As you become more successful as a rehabber, you may encounter houses that challenge your skills.

Here are a few pointers that I learned from my most challenging flip ever, which I call the Cat House:

- Don't buy houses sight unseen, unless you are very, very experienced.

- If you buy houses in other parts of the country, where you cannot see the house, ask a real estate agent or someone else to send photos showing the inside.

If you buy houses that are infested with animal odors:

- Remove drywall up to the level that animals have urinated.

- Wipe down the entire house including walls, ceilings, floors, and studs, with a germicide.

- Remove insulation in the ceiling and up to where you removed the sheet rock.

- Paint any remaining sheet rock, wood studs and floors with germicidal sealant paint. It cleans the house and seals it.

- Remove the interior air-conditioning unit and all air-conditioning duct work if necessary.

- Fog the house with a germicide.

weekends together going to the park or playing football.

Veronica and I love beaches. We love being near the ocean. But it had been years since we had visited one. Now, we could go on vacations. We lounged on the beach in Cancun, visited theme parks in California, and relaxed on cruise ships.

By winter 2004, I had perfected my systems. That's when the business really exploded, and I started flipping six to eight houses a month.

**Replace Yourself**

Create systems as a way to replace yourself in the business. This gives you more time to step away from the business, while increasing profits.

Systems duplicate processes so that others can do the same task over and over again. You can step away and know the job is getting done exactly as you want it.

If you set up your systems correctly, you can get this done without hiring employees. In the real estate business, you can easily hire people who get paid on commission to get work done. You can create your army of entrepreneurs by working with independent appraisers, real estate agents, loan processors, subcontractors and so on.

Remember, it is much more efficient to work with an army of small entrepreneurs than a cast of employees who are always looking to you for what to do next. If someone has enough pride to be in business for themselves, they will have enough pride to do a good job.

It is much easier to gamble on a painter as a subcontractor than as an employee. Frankly, it's good for them, the economy and the world of business for subcontractors to be self-employed.

**Paperwork Systems**

You can also create paperwork systems to manage your projects.

My paperwork system helps organize my projects to:

# Chapter 14

## Deals Everywhere
*My Business Overflows with Leads*

- **Rolling with Deals**
- **The House with Goats and Sheep**
- **The No-Mold Short Sale**
- **The Partnership Flip**
- **The Multi-House Package**
- **The Fishing Guy's Retreat**

### Rolling With Deals

I had built a very solid flipping machine by early 2004. It generated so many leads I was able to pick the cream of the crop. I busted the belief that deals were hard to find. I got on a roll and started finding deals everywhere.

By now, my flipping machine had eight ways to find deals and six ways to sell. I had developed a way to manage contractors. I created cookie-cutter methods for fix-up, generic product lists, and more than 10 ways to market the houses. Plus, I had a great team.

When I let enough people know that this is what I did, I got tons of referrals by word of mouth. There is always somebody who knows somebody who knows somebody who wants to get rid of a house. There are always people out there who need help.

- track offers
- manage orders for appraisals, loans, title and insurance
- handle contractors
- invoice contractors
- organize files
- track projects
- manage budgets

With systems, you spend less time with the business, and the business will keep generating cash.

## How to Manage Contractors

You want to manage contractors in a way that maximizes your profits.

If you are a giving person, you might be tempted to give contractors more money and more work. But just giving a contractor more money is not going to make them a better contractor. If someone is a bad contractor, giving them more money is like putting gum on a broken dam. You will not be able to prevent it from leaking.

A good contractor is a good contractor because he is a good, savvy businessperson. Build loyalty with your contractors by treating them fairly and paying them on time.

You need to negotiate good prices with your contractors so that you can make money on a deal. Once you can make profits, you will be able to flip more houses to give your contractors more work.

With a system in place, I had the strategies to put deals together easily. Once I gained momentum, deals just flowed.

## The House with Goats and Sheep

I met a woman who raised goats and sheep in her backyard. There were fleas everywhere, and the house stank.

The woman didn't like her house because it was on the corner of a major street, with a lot of traffic and noise. She also wanted to get out of San Antonio and live with her elderly mother on her ranch. A competitor who could not do the deal offered it to me.

I saw an opportunity here, so I offered to buy the house.

I told the woman I would buy the property, but on the condition that she would allow me to put up a "For Sale" sign immediately, while it was still under contract. She agreed. I bought the house for $60,000.

I decided to sell it on an owner-finance basis because I wanted to move it quickly. As soon as I put up the "For Sale – Owner Finance" sign, the office phone blew up with calls. Everyone was calling about this property.

One man who called was a mechanic, who said he wanted the space on the property for his shop. He also liked that the house was in the center of town, within five minutes of two major freeways.

"There are goats in the backyard," I said.

"I don't care about the animals in the backyard," he said. "It's not a big deal. I'll take care of that stuff. I love the house and I love the location, and I will buy it."

**Contractor Paperwork**

In my Flip and Grow Rich system, I use eight documents for working with contractors. These include:

- Budget Repair Sheet
- Subcontractor Agreement
- Subcontractor Invoicing Letter
- Kitchen Product Shopping List
- Bathroom Product Shopping List

The product shopping lists show exactly what model, brand, size and color of appliances and fixtures I purchase for every house.

These lists reduce the time and energy that is spent managing projects. It's another way to maximize profits.

He said he didn't have good credit, but that he made good money. "I have cash."

"We are selling the house for $100, 000," I said.

He said, "I'll give you $10,000 down."

I said, "OK, you can buy it on Friday, in a week and a half, after 3 p.m., because that's when I will own the property."

He came to my office that Friday at 5:30 p.m. with $10,000 in cash, exactly two and a half hours after I bought the property.

I sold it to him as an owner-finance deal and got $10,000, which I deposited in the bank. I wrote a mortgage note for the balance of $90,000. He would make monthly payments on this note.

The guy's credit was not as bad as he thought, which meant I could quickly sell the mortgage note to a bank that buys such notes.

A few weeks later, I sold the note at a 96 percent discount, for $86,400. That gave me a profit of $26,400 on the note. When the $10,000 down payment was added in, my total gross profit on the deal was $36,400.

Everyone was thrilled. The new homeowner was happy because I gave him a chance no one else would – to own a home. The note buyer was happy because the owner had put cash down on the property and they purchased a discounted mortgage note. And I, of course, was happy because I made $36,400 on a property that sold less than three hours after I bought it.

I also could have quickly sold the house through a real estate agent. But by selling to this buyer through owner financing, I didn't have to

# Chapter N

## Mentoring Others
How These Methods Can Work for Anybody

- **Coaching Students**
- **Theresa – In Debt and Pregnant**
- **Raymond – Paying Off the IRS**
- **Larry – the 72-Year-Old Retiree**
- **The Rewards**

### Coaching Students

The Flip and Grow Rich system that I have developed works for people from all walks of life.

Through my company's coaching program, I have successfully mentored thousands of students. The people I have taught come from a variety of backgrounds, but their reasons for wanting to flip houses are similar:

- Get out of debt
- Make more money
- Create alternatives to a job
- Build cash reserves
- Save for their children's future

put a single dollar into repairing it, and I didn't have to pay agent fees. If I sold the house through an agent, I would have had to put about $5,000 into fixing it up, which isn't much, but it still would have been work, and the real estate agent would still have to show it. Even if an agent sold the house in one day, I would have to pay real estate agent commissions. Instead, I took a discount on the note.

This way, I got a buyer the first day. I got $10,000 down immediately, and then 30 days later I got the rest of my money. It would have taken a conventional buyer's loan 30 days minimum to close, but I got paid upfront and again after a month. The best part was that I bought and sold the property on the same day.

I made really good money on this deal, and I didn't have to put a dime or any time into it.

## The No-Mold Short Sale

Sally had to choose between paying a mortgage on a house she did not want and sending her daughter to college.

She had recently bought a house. But the day she moved in, the neighbors told her the house had mold. She moved into an apartment the next day.

Sally was stretched. She was living on a teacher's salary, paying $1,000 a month mortgage for an empty house, plus another $1,000 per month rent for her apartment.

In addition, Sally was a single mom, with a daughter who was about to start college that fall. Sally would not have enough money to make two house payments and pay college tuition.

Her credit was still good, but her time was running out. If she could not pay, she would soon face foreclosure.

- Save for retirement
- Leave a family legacy

Their challenges in flipping houses are also similar:

- no cash
- no credit
- massive debt
- low-paying jobs
- no experience

Coaching is a way for me to give back. It's a way for me to fulfill my promise to Veronica that if I were successful, I would teach my secrets to others.

I have always mentored students over the phone. I do not need to go see houses with students. I give them sample documents and teach how to use them.

All my students do their own deals. When they make their profits, I do not require them to share those profits with me. My satisfaction is in seeing their dreams come true.

I started mentoring students in 2004, after people who heard me speak asked for guidance and real estate professionals began referring novice investors to me.

By 2007, I had trained an entire team of coaches to mentor thousands of students requesting the service. Each student receives individual coaching.

The house had very little equity, so she didn't have room to fix or sell it through a real estate agent. She owed $105,000 on a house worth $115,000 the year before.

Contractor and engineer estimates showed it would cost $45,000 to $60,000 to fix the mold problem. She did not have that kind of money, and the house was not worth that much.

I have seen a lot of houses with mold, and I told Sally that I did not see any mold in this one. But Sally insisted there was. She said she had an engineer's report proving it. She also had contractors' reports saying how much the repairs would be. And she refused to work with other investors who had told her there was no mold.

I decided it was pointless to try to convince her otherwise.

"I will turn those reports in to the bank, if you agree to sell it to me," I told Sally. She agreed.

So I sent those reports to the bank, and I offered $45,000 for the house. I told the bank that I would purchase the property within 14 days of their approving the dollar amount.

I explained Sally's situation to the bank. I said that Sally had good credit, but if she could not make the payments, the house would go into foreclosure. If the loan foreclosed, the bank would have to manage a home that Sally believed had mold, which would potentially cost them $45,000 to $60,000 to repair, according to the estimates, which were in the package.

The bank sent back a denial letter. They would not do a short sale, which meant discounting the price to less than what was owed on the mortgage.

I don't know what changed, but a week later, they accepted my offer

The following are just a few examples of students I have mentored and the deals they made.

### Theresa – In Debt and Pregnant

Theresa was pregnant and $35,000 in debt when she started flipping houses.

She and her husband had put their wedding expenses on credit cards. That was $25,000, which, including interest, had grown to $35,000. That put a lot of pressure on the marriage. She wanted to flip houses to pay off the debt.

Theresa was referred to me in 2004. She told me about a deal she had found that would have made a $5,000 profit.

I went over the numbers with her and said, "Don't do it. This is a bad deal." I explained that there is a difference between a discount and a deal. This was a discount. It did not leave enough margin for mistakes, budget overruns or profit. She backed off.

Soon after that, Theresa said she was still interested in real estate. "But I can't do it. I'm pregnant."

"What does that have to do with anything?" I asked.

"Well, I can't get the real estate deals done!" she said.

"Theresa," I said, "You don't need to be getting down on your hands and knees to lay tile or getting on a ladder to paint. I can teach you to do this, so you know all the tricks to get it done easier, faster and with a bigger profit."

of $45,000. The bank discounted the mortgage from $105,000 to $45,000. This is where I made my profit.

Sally could barely believe me when I told her the bank accepted my offer.

I put about $2,200 into it to clean the carpet and touch up the paint. Two months later, I sold the house for $128,000.

After I bought the property, I studied the reports more closely. The engineer's report was by a structural engineer who said there was a probability the house had mold. The contractors' reports were estimates based on if the house had mold. No one actually said the house had mold.

I brought in a microbiologist to take tests. He confirmed it. There was no mold in the house. I got a great deal, and Sally got to walk away from a bad situation.

## The Partnership Flip

I was approached by a man, Frank, who wanted to start a business flipping houses, but he did not know how. He also had a relative who was behind on property tax payments and needed to sell the property.

Frank and I agreed to become partners on the deal. I would take $5,000 up front for running the project, and he would learn how to flip houses. Then we would split the profits evenly.

I showed Frank how to put the loan in his name. Then at closing, we put the property in a corporation that I controlled.

We got a loan that covered the cost of the property, repairs and my upfront fee. That was for $42,000 for the property, $45,000 for repairs and my $5,000 fee. We purchased the property and I walked

She learned my methods and made about $35,000 on her first deal. She was able to clear all her debt. Was Theresa done? No. She flipped more houses. She soon had a goal of replacing her job. She planned to build a year's worth of living expenses as cash reserves first.

Theresa totally turned her life around.

### Raymond – Paying Off the IRS

Raymond met me through a friend of a friend. He was about 6 feet 2 inches tall, middle-aged, with long hair and a ragged face. When he spoke, he had such anxiety in his voice that it seemed he truly needed help.

When Raymond called me, he owed the IRS $27,000. He asked me to teach him how to flip houses, so he could use the profits to pay off the IRS. After that, he said, he wanted to get into real estate investing full time.

I taught him how to find a house to fix and flip. He made $42,000 on his first deal.

I advised him to use some of that money to pay a portion of the IRS bill, then save a chunk of it for the next deal. After he did another flip, he could use part of it to pay the remainder of the IRS bill.

Then Raymond did a second deal and made $24,000.

After that, he came back asking for help. He was frantic.

away from the buying table with $5,000 in my pocket.

I had the property repaired in approximately five weeks. Frank did not follow me around the entire time. In fact, he watched from a distance. However, he learned where to find money with no money out of his pocket, how to make the deal and sell the property. I also taught him more ways to find undervalued houses.

When the house sold, we split the profit of $45,000. I made $22,500 plus my $5,000 fee. This is not a lot of money for me, but it is not bad for five weeks of work.

For Frank, it launched his flipping career. Frank "paid" $27,500 for my services, earned $22,500 in cash, and got the education of his life.

He has since gone on to become a successful flipper. Last I spoke with him, he said he was flipping about 10 deals a year and only worked when he wanted. He made great money and spent the rest of his time on his hobbies.

For Frank, that $27,500 was a small price to pay for being able to live his dreams.

## The Multi-House Package

When I buy properties, I like to ask the sellers if they might have other houses for sale, or if they know of friends who might have houses for sale. You would think that if someone is in financial trouble, they only have one house for sale. You'd be surprised.

In summer 2006, I looked at one house with a real estate agent and we started chatting.

"Does your seller have any other houses they would like to sell?" I asked.

"I'm stressed out about money," he said. "I still have all these bills. The IRS is breathing down my neck."

"How could you be stressed out?" I said. "You made more than enough to pay off the IRS."

"Well, I didn't pay them," he said sheepishly.

"OK, but how much do you have left?" I asked.

"None," he said.

Raymond had spent all his profits on new things – a car, computer and cell phone for his son, who was so excited because it could take photos of a girl he liked.

When it was all done, Raymond had spent all of his $66,000 in profits from his first two deals. Now he had to start all over again.

"A girlfriend's face on a cell phone is not going to matter if the IRS throws you in jail," I said. "Of the $66,000 you made, you should have paid down $14,000 the first time and another $13,000 the second time. You would have had no IRS tax bill, and you would have had $39,000 to continue to grow your business."

"I should have listened to you the first time!" he said.

"And the second time," I said.

I knew I was laying it on, but I continued. "Look at me. I live a very modest lifestyle for the amount of money that I make. Why is that? Because I don't want to be walking around

Turns out the seller owned close to 100 properties. Her husband had recently passed away, and she planned to sell her houses one at a time over the next several years.

The houses were all paid off. The woman was receiving a nice residual monthly income on the rentals. Some of the houses needed a lot of repairs. Some didn't need any.

The lady was a smart negotiator and a savvy businesswoman. She wanted to keep the profitable houses and sell me the ones with no profit. However, I knew one thing for sure: if I solved her problem I could make a good deal.

So we negotiated for about two weeks before we put it under contract. She was already a multimillionaire. The negotiation was more a game for her than a necessity.

Ultimately, she sold me the cream-of-the-crop houses and kept the rest for a tax write-off. She wanted too much money for the amount of repairs on the deals with no profit. After the sale, she said, she was extremely happy because she wanted to travel the world and buy a new Rolls-Royce. Funny problem to have, but I helped her solve it.

My partners and I did it with no money out of pocket. We went through four hard-money lenders. Due to the complexity of the deals, I purchased several dozen of her properties over a period of two months, which is longer than my standard 14 days for one house.

We got the whole package for 55 cents on the dollar. We spent $1.08 million for all the houses, which were worth $1.95 million fixed up. We put in about $200,000 in repairs for all the houses. This was definitely a home run project, as we netted $600,000 in profits.

It was one of the largest packages I ever closed.

stressed out every day. I do this business to have less stress in my life, not more."

"I just felt like getting something nice," Raymond said.

"That's what drug dealers do," I said. "They go out and spend a ton of money on lifestyle, then they don't have money left over."

Raymond sobered up.

After that, I taught him how to do some quick paper flips, like the first deal I had ever done. That way, he would make less of a profit, but he would have money in his pocket sooner.

Raymond made $8,000 on the next deal and $22,000 on the one after that. He paid down half the IRS bill and kept the rest for working capital.

I don't respect that Raymond spent his profits the wrong way. But I do give him credit for getting off his butt and flipping houses.

Even though Raymond screwed up, he still made money because of the simple methods I taught him. Some people are slower than others, but even slow people eventually learn.

### Larry – the 72-Year-Old Retiree

In early 2006, I was invited to speak to a group of investors about how I created so much real estate wealth in such a short time. This was my first time speaking about real estate in front of an audience and I did not know what to expect.

After we fixed them up, my partners and I sold some of those houses, kept some of them as rentals and split the assets.

## The Fishing Guy's Retreat

A friend of a friend referred me to a gentleman named Gene.

Gene lived in a small town outside San Antonio. He owned an apartment complex near the coast, where he liked to fish on the weekends.

He had invested in real estate most of his life. In recent years, he had sold off about 30 properties and planned to use the money for retirement. He now had just two rental properties left that he wanted to keep for cash flow.

But then his wife, Kathy, was diagnosed with cancer. Her operation would cost $100,000, and they did not qualify for insurance.

Gene had owned the building for 30 years. He kept it in great shape and it was paid off. It had nine units, fully rented, except for one that he kept to store his fishing gear.

Gene and I spent three hours together driving to the property. We talked the whole way. He told me everything I needed to know about fishing and other things I didn't need to know.

We got there and walked the grounds. The property was worth $200,000.

If Gene tried to sell it at market value, listing the building through a real estate agent, it might take several months before a potential buyer made an offer. Then it could be another one to two months before the buyer qualified for a loan and closed. The whole process

I asked the organizer what the typical attendance was for this monthly event. She said about 40 people. However, because I had built such a large real estate empire and was still running the business, in contrast with speakers who were just selling a program, she said I had a lot more legitimacy. They expected a big turnout.

That night, some 200 people attended the talk.

I spoke for an hour, and when I was finished, I received a standing ovation. About a quarter of the crowd rushed up, asking me to teach them real estate investing. When I saw the eager – and sometimes anxious – look in people's eyes, I was truly moved to teach.

However, because of my schedule, I could take on only one student at a time.

One student I accepted was Larry, a 72-year-old retiree. He had some savings, but wanted to create enough income to last for the rest of his years.

I liked Larry because he did not act 72, but more like 22. I could relate to him. In the past, when people would condescendingly ask, "When are you going to grow up?" I would answer, "This is as good as it gets."

Over the course of a year, I showed Larry how to create real estate riches beyond what he originally thought was possible.

The following is a direct quote from Larry as he was in the middle of closing several deals.

could last six months – and by then, it might be too late for his wife.

Gene did not want to tap into his retirement savings for the operation. And keeping the building for cash flow now would not yield enough to pay for it. So he was motivated to sell.

I asked, "How much do you need for your wife's operation?"

"$100,000," he said.

"I'll pay $100,000 for it," I said.

He said, "I'm OK with that. I know you're getting a heck of a deal. But my wife needs surgery now, and I don't have time for somebody to go out there and get a loan."

Three weeks later, we closed.

Gene was extremely grateful and we built up a great relationship. The day after we closed, he drove down to the property to fix a storm door. The renters had damaged it, and he wanted me to have a perfect property. I spent zero dollars on repairs. The property was in fantastic condition.

I kept it as a rental. I could easily have flipped it, but the cash flow was worth keeping. Each unit had a market rent value of $400 a month, so total potential income was $3,600 a month. The mortgage was $1,000, so I had a potential cash flow of $2,600 a month before taxes.

Gene had rented the units below market rates for 30 years. Now, that difference was my profit center. All I had to do was raise rents and the complex was an instant cash cow.

"I am 72 years old and wanted to secure my retirement years with good income. By using Armando's system, I have purchased three properties and have a profit of $45,000. I also have four more deals under contract with $750,000 worth of profit. Now I have the security I wanted and I am having the most fun I've ever had."

Shortly after writing this, Larry closed on all those deals. He became the owner of all those properties.

## The Rewards

I get a lot of satisfaction from helping people learn to flip houses. I like helping people fulfill their life dreams, just as flipping has done for me.

Several early students offered me a slice of their profits as a thank you. But I told them to keep it – they had done the deal. The fact that they did it earned my respect, and that was worth more than their money. I want to see people standing on their feet, paying off debt, taking care of their kids, planning for their future. That was satisfying enough.

Due to the popularity of my television show, public demand for my system has led me to put my flipping system into an educational format. I have created several programs to teach my system.

I have put together a coaching team of experienced investors. We have taught thousands of students how to generate wealth. Together, we offer my Flip and Grow Rich program, which

Two years later, I saw Gene and Kathy, at a restaurant. They were enjoying their retirement now, traveling across the United States.

Kathy was in good health. She thanked me and said the operation had saved her life. Gene also thanked me because he still had his wife of 50 years.

When someone thanks you from the bottom of their heart for helping to save their life, it's such a proud moment. Beyond the money, real estate is a great business because it's a people business.

includes workshops, seminars, coaching, manuals, CDs and books.

To reach my coaches, contact:
1-800-771-6202 x 4001 or www.armandocoaching.com

My system catapulted my own business. My system works for others, too. It can be successfully duplicated and used by many people.

But early on, I learned that I do not want to teach people to flip houses so that they can burn through capital. My inspiration comes from teaching people to change their lives.

# Chapter 15

## Enjoying the Wealth
### *Sharing My Abundance*

- **Buying Whatever I Want**
- **Lifestyle of Athletes**
- **Vacations**
- **Thanking My Family**
- **Our Dream Home**
- **I Had Arrived**

### Buying Whatever I Want

By June 2004, I was consistently flipping more than five houses a month. My business had gotten to the point where the thought of money no longer sent me into a downward spiral of worry.

At this point, I could buy whatever I wanted and go on vacation whenever I wanted. You would think that I would want to buy motorcycles, yachts, mansions and jewelry.

But that's not what I wanted.

There are many people who have nice things, but they're living month to month. I no longer needed to impress people.

When I started in the business, I needed to feed my family, house them, get out of debt and build a cushion. I wanted large cash

# Chapter 0

## How to Get Rich
Keep Your Fountain of Wealth Flowing

- **How Much to Invest**
- **Investments Before Luxury**
- **Five Levels of Earning Income**
- **Use Money to Make Money**
- **How to Manage Your Profits**
- **When to Quit Your Job**
- **The Path to True Wealth**
- **The Path to True Lifestyle**

### How Much to Invest

No matter how much money you make, you have to regularly analyze:

- how much to spend
- how much to save
- how much to reinvest

Many investors teach you to reinvest 10 percent of your income, because it's doable and attainable. Ten percent is a great starting point, but I believe the ideal amount to reinvest is 40 percent

reserves. Now that I had it, I could let my money make more money for me. I wanted to build a wide, deep wealth, and real estate was the way to go.

I started accumulating massive amounts of rental and commercial properties. That was the retirement program. Rental properties gave me tax benefits. Commercial buildings gave me depreciation breaks.

What I wanted was more real estate.

## Lifestyle of Athletes

I learned something about financial management from a friend. He is a financial analyst for professional athletes.

He told me about what happens with many of these athletes. The typical professional athlete has a career lifespan of about three to five years. During that time, the average guy makes up to $8 million a year.

"You know how he spends that money?" my buddy asked.

"How?" I replied.

"Here's how it breaks down," he said. "Based on an average $8 million per player, $4 million goes to taxes, managers and agent fees. He will spend $2.5 million to $3 million on lifestyle. Maybe he'll save $1 million to $1.5 million. For most people, that's a lot of money."

"Sure," I nodded.

"But for someone who only has a five-year playing career, that's only $5 million. And he is used to making $8 million a year," he said. "You know what's going to happen?"

of your income. As long as you're not gambling and not being a complete imbecile, you should be able to become very rich by reinvesting 40 percent of your income.

It's tough to invest that much of your paycheck. However, if you are flipping and making the big dollars, you need to build the habit of saving and investing 40 percent to 50 percent of your profits. As you save money, you will be amazed by the opportunities that come your way to make even more money.

### Investments Before Luxury

While you begin to flip real estate and make more money, you may be tempted to spend more on luxury lifestyle items. You start buying boats, cars, jewelry and other luxuries.

When building your financial empire – whether you're building a small empire making $50,000 a year or a large empire making several million dollars a year flipping houses – never get caught up in lifestyle before your real estate investments can generate enough cash reserves to reinvest. Don't flip a property, make $30,000 and buy a new car. That's not the purpose of flipping houses.

What you want is peace of mind. It goes back to having balance in life. It goes back to being able to relax. You want to know that you'll wake up the next day because you enjoy making money, not because you have to pay the bills. If you make an extra $30,000 or $300,000 and you start spending it on cars, jewelry and clothes, you are still going to be strapped. You will be stressed. Your life will not be any different than it is now earning a paycheck and struggling to make ends meet.

"What?"

"He goes broke," the planner said. "And then he's not going to have the lifestyle he wants."

I was silent.

"But if the athlete spends his money strategically, he could be in a different situation," my friend said. "Let's say he still has $4 million in taxes and agent fees. Then maybe he spends $600,000 on lifestyle. And the rest he reinvests. So he has $3.4 million set aside each year. At the end of five years, he's got $20 million invested, and he could be worth $30 million to $40 million."

When I heard this, I knew I was on the right track.

So rather than spend my money on more cars, jewelry and all that crazy stuff, I spend my money on real estate. I have purchased some nice houses, and we are starting to buy second homes on beaches. I buy rental properties and commercial properties. Everything I buy is paid for by my investments.

## Vacations

By 2004, I started taking more vacations with my family. What we really wanted as a family was not more possessions, but more time together. So that's what we did.

We visited beaches, went on road trips and enjoyed long cruises. We took our son to see wild alligators, rode hoverboats in Florida's swamps and flew to isolated beach resorts in places such as Ixtapa, Mexico.

It's unfortunate, but the American middle class way of life is to buy things on monthly payment plans. The wealthy way is to make enough money and have your investments feed your lifestyle. That way, you are not working for your money. Your money works for you. You feed your lifestyle by having large cash reserves.

## SPENDING YOUR FLIPPING PROFITS ON LUXURIES SENDS YOU BACK TO THE PAYCHECK TREADMILL

We took driving trips across the U.S. We would pick up my son after school in the summer and take off for a week. He loves roller coasters, so we took him to theme parks across the country. We went to Six Flags, SeaWorld, Disneyland, Disney World and Knott's Berry Farm. We were constantly doing things with him.

In all those places, we also looked at real estate. We contacted property agents on those trips and wrote off the trip. We stopped calling them vacations. We called them working trips.

I know a lot of people who take out loans or max out their credit cards to go on vacation. But we did not have to go into debt. We were staying at the best hotels and paying cash.

There's real estate everywhere. It's tax deductible. When you're a real estate investor, you can write off vacations.

Now, we typically go on working trips about once a quarter, for seven to 10 days at a time.

When we're back at home, I also have more time for my family. We go to the zoo or the playground. I take Mondo Man to play football and soccer. We do things that kids like to do.

### Thanking My Family

I also used our wealth to thank my family.

I repaid Veronica's father the money I lost when our condo in California was foreclosed. I repaid my father the loan for moving across the country. We also helped our family and relatives financially.

I also invited one of my brothers and his wife to join me in the

**Five Levels of Earning Income**

As you grow, you go through different stages of earning, which I call the Five Levels of Earning Income.

Five Levels of Earning Income

1. Unemployment – You have no income.
2. Employment – You earn money by working for someone else.
3. Self-employment – You earn money by working for yourself or your business.
4. Entrepreneurship – Your business makes money for you.
5. Profit regeneration – Your money makes money for you.

You make good money when you're self-employed. You start making great money when you're an entrepreneur. But you start getting rich when your money makes money.

If you use other people's money to go into entrepreneurship, their money will make you money.

Maybe you are unemployed or employed. Your income is limited to what your boss pays you. Maybe you are self-employed. Your small business may be nothing more than a well-paid job.

If you don't spend your money on lifestyle and keep investing it, you will reach a point where your money will make you money. It's hard to create cash reserves for profit regeneration unless you regularly have large cash infusions. Flipping houses can give you those large cash infusions.

business. I wanted to share the wealth with them, and it was fun to work together.

## Our Dream Home

In June 2004, Veronica and I moved into our dream home.

It was 4,100 square feet, with Italian marble floors, marble fireplace, a wet bar and a beautiful, large, enclosed swimming pool. When we moved in, we furnished it with amazing leather furniture, which was made in the style of kings and queens. We felt like royalty.

Of course, we purchased the house at a discount. We bought it for 40 cents on the dollar. It was run-down, and we took six months to fix it up.

I bought the house the way I bought many of my deals. I met the homeowners through their lawyer, who had helped them sue the insurance company. The underinsured house had suffered water damage and mold. When I met the homeowners, I listened to their story – how they had raised their children here and how the damage happened; how the insurance company did not cover the expenses and the family ultimately just wanted to move on.

"But we don't want to just give it to anybody," the husband said. "We want people who will care about it as much as we have."

"My wife, my son and I will move into this house," I told him. "I'll raise my family here, like you have raised your family."

On June 21, 2004, after everything had been fixed up, we moved in. At one point, I just stood in the dining room, taking it all in. Veronica was in her nesting mode, making the place all warm and cozy.

### Use Money to Make Money

If you are flipping houses and spending all your profits on lifestyle, you will have a more luxurious lifestyle. But now you're just a well-paid, self-employed person.

## Leapfrogging from Unemployment to Profit Regeneration

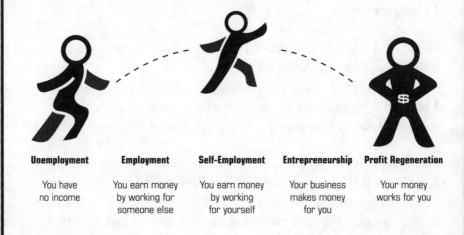

| Unemployment | Employment | Self-Employment | Entrepreneurship | Profit Regeneration |
|---|---|---|---|---|
| You have no income | You earn money by working for someone else | You earn money by working for yourself | Your business makes money for you | Your money works for you |

If you are an entrepreneur reinvesting your profits or using profit regeneration, your business and your investments work for you, and your money will always make more money than you can. That's when you start building cash reserves.

Don't spend your money on lifestyle goods until you have large cash reserves. A minimum cash reserve is one year's worth of savings, enough for you to live on if you do not have a job. Again, do not use this cash reserve on improving your lifestyle; focus on reinvesting and creating residual income.

My son was running around, checking everything out. He was five years old. He had so much room to play. He looked back at me and gave me a face of contentment. He ran over to me, gave me a big hug and ran off again.

At that moment, I breathed a sigh of satisfaction. I finally felt that I was a good provider.

## I Had Arrived

I felt like I had arrived. I could accomplish anything I wanted. And I didn't have to be afraid of anything again.

I had kept my promise to give my wife an amazing life. I felt successful, because my family felt content and we deserved it.

I realized it was only three years ago that we were living in a garage. It was exactly three years ago, in late June, that I made the big decision to upgrade our lives. If I had not been brave in the face of fear, we might not have moved out of the garage and returned to San Antonio in August 2001.

If I had not listened to my gut, I would not have known this feeling of success. I would not have known how great my life could be. My son would probably be disappointed with me.

Now, I was moving my family into this dream home. I had lived up to my capabilities and I felt very proud. Now, I could create new dreams based on helping more people.

People talk about making a couple of hundred dollars residual income through stocks and rental properties. But you can create exponential growth by having residual income off your cash reserves. Then you are using a portion of your cash reserves for flipping.

You can take $50,000 in cash reserves, buy three houses and make payments on those loans. You would make triple your cash reserves flipping houses, versus spending $50,000 on lifestyle.

Now what's happening is you're using your money to make money. By flipping houses, you can jump from unemployment – leapfrog over employment, self-employment and entrepreneurship – and land at profit regeneration, so your money works for you.

### How to Manage Your Profits

My recommendation is that you take not just 40 percent, but 50 percent of the money you earn and save it. Then use the other 50 percent to reinvest in future flips.

Do not use all your investment money to do one flip. Split your money to make down payments on two or three properties. Borrow the remainder of the loans from hard-money lenders. By leveraging your money, you can buy two or three properties at a time, not just one. And you will have a backup, because half of the money is still in reserve.

Now you're following the formula taught in *The Richest Man in Babylon*, by George S. Clason. In that book, he says to invest at

# Chapter 16

## Landing the TV Show
*Daring to Dream Big*

- **Pipe Dream**
- **The Application**
- **The Producer Flies Out**
- **The Wait**
- **The Stand-In Actor's House**
- **The Launch Party**
- **Mondo Man's Night**

### Pipe Dream

In 2005, my company really started taking off. The number of houses we flipped each month tripled from eight in January to 25 in December.

When I told other rehabbers our numbers, they were stunned. Even the most experienced of investors wanted to know how I was getting my deals and flipping so many properties.

By this stage, I had expanded my full-time staff to nine people. This included a secretary, office manager, loan processor, two buyers, two sellers and me. Now that Mondo Man was going to school, Veronica joined the business as a sales associate. She quickly became the best sales associate I knew.

least 10 percent of your income. You are doing that by investing in flipping houses.

I believe investing 40 percent of your income is the ideal mark to create massive wealth, but you must start somewhere, even if it is only 10 percent. As you increase your income, you can move to the ideal 40 percent mark.

These laws are created by truth. Truth never changes. Money has laws like gravity. Spend money like crazy and you will fall on your face. Reinvest it wisely and you will have profit regeneration, which will make you wealthy even if you make mistakes.

## When to Quit Your Job

People often ask if they should quit their jobs to flip houses full time. That's not my recommendation to most people.

My recommendation for people who want to quit their job is to build up enough cash that is equal to one year of income. Do that by keeping your job and flipping at the same time. Once you have acquired one year's worth of savings equal to the amount of money you would have made from your job, then you can quit.

Understand, I am not telling you to quit your job. Some people might prefer to keep their job, earn that income and then add to it by flipping houses. That is also a great way to build a fortune.

This is not about "flip and grow stress." This is about "flip and grow rich." This is about quality of life. Before quitting your job,

In addition to this, we had a huge list of subcontractors working for us, each with their own crew of three to four guys. I had a title company, lawyer and a certified public accountant on our team. We were a full-blown company.

Since it was the turn of the year, I thought it would be good for our staff to set goals for the year. Veronica and I hosted a breakfast at our house, and everybody came over.

I believe that writing down goals keeps us focused and motivates us to succeed. I invited everyone to write goals for all areas of their life. This way, they would not feel that they were just working for a paycheck. I asked them to list their dreams for their lives, finances, time and vacations.

I asked everyone to dream as if anything is possible, as if they could achieve anything, like a little kid might do. This is because I believe true inspiration comes from our unconscious mind. That's how we get our best ideas. We only crush our dreams with our fear.

I was in this inspired mode when I also started writing down my goals. I thought about all our staff, our contractors, lenders, seller and buyers – all these crazy people and our crazy business. I had seen some really stupid reality TV shows, and I thought that what we do is awesome. Then it all came together and I wrote down another goal.

We went around the room, with each person sharing their goals, and all of us supporting one another. Then came my turn.

"You know what would be interesting?" I said. "We could do our own reality TV show about our business."

No one said anything. They were in shock. Then they sort of mumbled, "Uh, OK. That's interesting."

I put my goal list in my office desk drawer. I would look at it from

go back to your "why" and think about which course of action will get you to your outcome in the quickest and most safe way.

My recommendation is for people to build up enough savings to live for at least one year – ideally five years – without working. Then, you can start acquiring rental properties. That's because rental properties can cost a lot of money, especially when you have vacancies. I recommend that people have large cash reserves first.

This is about reducing stress. It's about freedom.

time to time, and I sometimes laughed. I focused on building a great company. I believed that by making a great company, we would create great opportunities for ourselves.

## The Application

In February 2006, I got a call from a lender with whom I had recently completed a deal.

"I just got contacted by someone in New York," he said. "They're looking for people to be on a TV show about real estate investors, rehabbers. That's not really my thing. But I thought you might want to call them."

I called the casting director in New York that Monday, and they e-mailed me an application.

The show was called "Flip This House," which airs on the A&E channel. It's a one-hour reality show featuring a real estate investor who rehabs houses. The network was looking for a new cast to fill the slot.

The irony was that after being so successful, I was actually afraid to fill out this application. It was something I wanted really badly, so I did not want to be disappointed by not getting it. However, I knew I had to follow my dreams.

When I checked my e-mail, I found an eight-page application. I was excited, but uncertain. I closed the door and turned off my cell phone.

I sat at my desk and read the application. I stared at it for two hours. I was no longer excited. I was scared. I had not felt fear like that in five years. Here I was, an extremely positive guy, and I was facing one

**The Path to True Wealth**

This is how I see the path to true wealth:

# Flip for Profits

  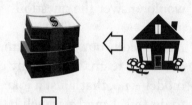

# Build Cash Reserves

# Profit Regeneration

# Balance

# Financial, Emotional, Time

# True Wealth

of my greatest fears. This is what I had wanted for so long, and I was terrified.

Then I remembered one of my mottos: "The things I fear the most, I must do."

I remembered my childhood dream of being a good businessman and being known for it. I thought that perhaps this was the time to fulfill the final part of my childhood dream. As I leaned forward, I read the application and wondered what the producers wanted and how I would answer the questions.

As I filled it out, I told them about my successes, my failures and our crazy team. "One of my crew members used to be an underwear model – no, that's just a joke," I wrote. I figured that if I was going to do this, I might as well have some fun. I told them about the time a squatter started living in one of our houses, and I threatened to let my Rottweiler go after him. I wanted to be a real guy. I wanted to show that I could sometimes be a knucklehead.

It took me six hours to fill out the application. I finally sent it in the next day, on Tuesday. On Wednesday, I got a call. "We really liked your application," said the assistant producer. "Can you make a DVD of yourself and send it in by Saturday?"

## The Producer Flies Out

That day, I called my subcontractors. I wanted all my guys to work on one house on Thursday. I wanted to shoot us flipping a house in one day.

On Thursday, we had 40 subcontractors show up at one house. It was a riot. We did chants. We screamed and danced. We were going full blast.

**The Path to True Lifestyle**

This is my definition of lifestyle: "The ability to live where you want, dress the way you want and drive what you want, while still having time for your life's passions and the ability and desire to contribute to causes greater than yourself."

Here's a simple lifestyle test for you:

1. Do you have enough income to comfortably reinvest 10 percent to 20 percent?

2. Do you make enough to comfortably live in the home of your dreams?

3. Do you make enough to comfortably drive the car you most desire?

4. Are you and your family taking vacations that leave long-lasting memories?

5. Do you have the time to spend with those you care about most?

6. Do you have the time to follow your passions?

7. Are you calling your own shots in life?

8. Do you give back to your community?

If you are answering "no" to all the above questions, you may not be living the lifestyle you desire and deserve to live. If this comment doesn't sit well with you and causes you discomfort, then I believe I am doing my job. You need to first realize where you are financially, so you can learn how to get to where you want to be.

At lunchtime, I got a call. It was one of the TV producers in New York. "Stop shooting the DVD," he said.

My heart sank.

He continued: "We're sending a producer out tomorrow. We want to see how you look on camera."

After I hung up the phone, I told Veronica and the crew. We all started shouting and screaming in celebration.

The next night, a producer named Andrew flew in.

They filmed us for two days. I took them to house after house after house that I had just bought, started rehabbing, just finished rehabbing or put on the market for sale. I showed Andrew the easiest flips and the most challenging flips. They filmed me directing my contractors, managing my team, visiting houses and negotiating with a homeowner. They taped personal interviews of each of us on the team.

The producer loved it. He said the most challenging houses created natural drama. He also saw that we had such a steady flow of deals that there would be no problem creating enough episodes to film.

On Saturday, we took Andrew out on the town. We wanted to show him that the Montelongos not only flip a lot of houses, but we have a blast doing it, too. We treated him to a Texas-style dinner.

We went crazy. We had drinks and told him, "If you're in Texas, you gotta have a Texas pickle." Texas pickles are huge – and hot – jalapeños. He took a bite and his face turned bright red.

"This is what we are about!" I yelled.

# Chapter P

## Set Your Goals
You Can Achieve Your Biggest Dreams

- **Follow Your Dreams**
- **Write Down Your Goals**
- **Business Checkups**
- **Face Your Fears**
- **Have Fun!**

### Follow Your Dreams

Your dreams, thoughts and desires permeate your brain. Even as you read these words, they are there.

You may be trying to change the channel in your mind, because you don't think your dreams are possible. Those dreams also will be challenged by people who don't want to share your dreams or who have given up on their own.

People may put down your dreams because it creates fear in them. They may think you are going to change or that their relationship with you is going to change. But understand that if you quit – if you do not chase your dreams and you let somebody else's fear stop you – then you are making a

## The Wait

Two weeks later, Andrew called. "We're interviewing 400 companies," he said. "We like you, but the problem is that you're really nice people. We're not sure if you have enough edge."

"I'm nice," I said, "but I also get pissed off. I was on my best behavior because you're one of the producers. What did you expect?"

I called his boss, Max, the show's executive producer and owner of the production company.

"If you don't hire me, you guys are crazy!" I told him. "Everyone else you're looking at f***ing sucks! I'm the best guy for the show! I out-work everybody, I out-hustle everybody, and if you want a guy with a f***ing edge, I will give you a f*** edge."

Lucky for me, Max is a seasoned and talented producer who saw my competitiveness and passion as a plus for the show and not a negative. Today, Max has my deepest respect and I believe I have his.

However, I wanted them to know I can be real and make fun of myself, but when it comes to getting the job done, there is no one better at the business, even if I have to be a jerk!

I got the show.

## The Stand-In Actor's House

I found out later what really tipped the TV producer. It was how I had bought a house from a woman during a negotiation they had filmed.

decision out of fear. And a decision made out of fear is always the wrong decision.

When I told people my dream of creating a reality show out of the flipping business, no one thought it was possible. They thought it was pie in the sky. But the desire stayed in my mind. Who in the world would have thought that I could be on TV and have the ability to touch millions of people because I flip houses and make money doing it?

Whatever you dream about accomplishing, those dreams can come true.

### Write Down Your Goals

What you believe is unachievable today is a dream waiting to happen tomorrow. All you have to do is start.

Write down your goals to focus your mind and make them happen more quickly. Even if your dreams seem impossible, write them down anyway.

Here's an exercise to help make your dreams come true:

Close your eyes.

Think about your dreams.

**Categorize your dreams in these major areas:**

- Financial
- Career
- Relationships

The woman was selling her father's house. Her father had been in the movies, acting as a stand-in for Errol Flynn, known for his romantic, swashbuckler roles in the 1940s. The woman's father also was a gun collector and photographer. The house was dated, but it showcased his taste and style, including antique light fixtures, classic sinks and faucets, and hand-laid tile in the bathroom.

Her father had passed away recently, and she had flown in from Utah to sell the house. She was in town for only two days and she wanted to make a deal. One of my competitors had called with the lead.

I met the woman at the house along with the TV producer and cameraman. As she showed us around, I could see how proud she was of her father's accomplishments. But she also was sad to let go of his home.

When we were looking at the hall bathroom, we started talking.

 "What can I do for you?" I asked.

"I don't know," she said. "I just don't want the memory of my father to go away."

"It seems to me that he lived a very active, passionate life," I said. "He was an actor, a writer, a photographer."

She nodded.

"This house is something that your father was really proud of," I said. "I promise to keep your father's signature in the house. I will make sure all those details stay, because that's exactly what he would have wanted."

She started to cry.

- Health
- Education
- Leisure
- Spiritual
- Other

**Write down your goals:**

For example:
- Financial – To have "X" dollars in the bank by "Y" date. To have "XX" dollars in assets by "YY" date.
- Education – Take a real estate course this month.
- Other – To sail around the world.
- Etc.

**GOALS:**

_____

_____

_____

_____

_____

_____

_____

_____

_____

_____

"I will keep the memory of your father alive," I said softly. "I will leave a lasting impression of him in the house."

She nodded. And she sold the house to me.

Ultimately, it came down to solving her problem. For me, it was not just about being on TV. It was about doing what I have always done – solving people's problems. When we serve others, we serve ourselves.

I kept my promise to that woman. When it was done, the rehabbed house still had some of the original fixtures that her father had installed.

The producers loved it. "You're a caring person," they said. "You connect with these people."

What actually appeared on the show was a very condensed version. Most of the footage ended up on the cutting floor. But it all boiled down to giving the homeowner what she wanted.

That flip became the first episode of our show. The producers called it: "The Movie-Star House."

## The Launch Party

Not everyone thought the show was a good idea. I got a lot of resistance from some people in the company. They thought we should concentrate on flipping houses, not get into the TV business.

But I had this thought: "If a lot of people think it's a bad idea, it's probably a good idea." In business, if you go against the popular myths, you're going to do well. I knew I was on the right track with the show.

Understand that making money can help you accomplish your goals and your dreams. Flipping can help you make that money.

Set your real estate goals.

Write down:

1. Date by when you will purchase your first or next flip.

2. Date by when you will finish fixing this house.

3. Date by when you will sell it.

4. Goal of how many flips you want to do in the next 12 months.

5. Amount of money you will make in the next 12 months flipping houses.

6. What you will do to continue your real estate education.

Put a copy of this list in several places:

- next to your bed
- on your lamps
- on your nightstand
- and on your mirror

Look at this page every day, so you keep your dreams in the forefront of your mind.

Veronica supported me. "If you think this is good for our business, if you think it's good for our lives, I'll follow you 100 percent," she said, "because I know it's one of your dreams."

Our first show was set to air on Sunday, July 23, 2006. We planned to throw a huge premiere party. We invited everyone in town – partners, bankers, hard-money lenders, business leaders, political leaders. The producers from New York also were flying in for the party. We probably had close to 400 people on the guest list.

We had restaurants, vendors, local radio and TV stations promoting the show. San Antonio had never been featured on a national TV series before, and this was a big deal for the entire city.

We had not seen the episode, so we were going to watch our show for the first time along with everyone else in town. I was very excited. How often does a person get applause after five years of hard work? It was a huge pat on the back.

## Mondo Man's Night

The Saturday before the big launch party, Veronica, Mondo Man and I went shopping. Veronica bought a dress, shoes and jewelry. Mondo Man and I got suits and ties.

Then we went to a casual restaurant with Veronica's parents, my niece and nephew. Mondo Man ordered a hamburger, and we all had the usual fare. We were excited about the launch party.

We got home and went to bed. Two hours later, Mondo Man started throwing up. He had diarrhea and vomited several times throughout the night. We were extremely worried.

## Business Checkups

Monitor your business by doing a checkup at least once a month. Make sure your dreams, financial goals and work ethic are aligned with one another.

I give myself a business checkup every week. I am my own biggest competitor, so I want to make sure I'm aligned in all areas. This allows me to move at a speed that most people cannot keep up with. You do not have to work at that kind of speed, but you want to be aligned.

These are the questions to ask for a business checkup:

- What are my dreams?
- What are my financial goals?
- Is my work ethic living up to my potential?
- What have I done this week to move towards accomplishing my dreams?

## Face Your Fears

What you fear the most is what you must do. Write down your top two fears when it comes to becoming successful at flipping houses.

In my experience, I find that people fear two things:

1. Failure
2. Success

The funny thing is people are more afraid of success than failure. But you can overcome both by taking action.

We took Mondo Man to the hospital in the morning. The doctors said he had food poisoning. They pumped fluids into him, and he kept throwing up and having diarrhea throughout the day.

By midafternoon, people were calling saying how excited they were about the party that night. "I don't know if we're gonna make it," I said. "If Mondo Man isn't better, we're not going."

The party was supposed to start at 6 p.m. By 5 p.m., people were asking if we were going to make it to our own party. Veronica and I decided not to go. "Our son is sick," I told them. "He's our family. He's our number one priority."

The show was slated to air at 8 p.m. We thought we could watch it at the hospital. But the hospital had only closed-circuit television and did not get the A&E channel.

Mondo Man knew what was going on. "Mom and Dad," he said. "It's your party, you can go. You don't have to stay here. I'll be OK."

Veronica and I looked at each other, and we had tears in our eyes. I leaned over and gave him a big hug.

"Son," I said, "the reason we are doing any of this stuff is because of you. The reason I have this show, the reason I work so much, the reason for all of this – is you. None of this means anything compared to you."

Veronica and I piled into his hospital bed with him and we spent the evening with the most important person in our lives.

"We don't care about the show right now," I said. "We like the show, but we love you more. We love you more than anything."

You can overcome fear by doing just one little thing, whether it's calling a real estate agent, checking the Internet for leads or calling a mentor.

Taking just one step will kickstart your brain to success. Even the smallest action will focus your mind, so that you're no longer thinking about fear. The fear in your mind will be replaced by new thoughts of action. With more action, these thoughts then become habits, which breed more success.

You can anchor this success with new strategies, systems and a mentor. This will give you fuel to achieve your goals and dreams. Overcoming fear of success is trickier because most people don't recognize it in themselves.

To overcome fear of success, you can try this short exercise. Remember a time in your life that you succeeded at something and truly surprised yourself. Remember the joy, excitement and pride you felt. Then remember what happened afterwards. Were you let down somehow? Most people fear success because they do not want to be disappointed. They do not think they can sustain the success. But were you in fact harmed? For most people, the answer is no.

The way to overcome this fear of success – or fear of disappointment – is by taking daily action. In fact, just by reading this book, you have started taking action. I applaud you for taking this first step. And you must remember that this book is just the first step.

Many people have read many books and done nothing with their knowledge. Don't be a passive reader. Be a doer! Just as when you were an infant you still needed guidance after taking your first step, you will need mentorship to grow your house

Mondo Man had a deep look of satisfaction. We all hugged each other for a long time.

Even though we missed the launch party, we had something more important: our family. It was an amazing night.

flipping skills after reading this book. As you continue to take action, you will be moving towards building a real estate fortune.

## Have Fun!

Each day you will be presented with many new challenges and options in your flipping business. However, at the end of each day, you will feel a huge sense of accomplishment.

It is exciting. No day is exactly alike. You're constantly learning, changing and maneuvering, but at the same time, you wake up energized.

The key to success is to have fun doing it. Always take your money, budgets and time frames very seriously. Do not take the people that you work with too seriously – and never take yourself too seriously.

The key to staying young is to have fun. The key to staying young – not immature – in business is to have fun in your business. As you gain experience, you want to maintain a fresh, young mindset. This is vital for your business health. You accomplish this by staying in an eager learning mode. Learning creates growth, and growth creates wealth.

When you have a system in place (I, of course, recommend using the best system – my system), you are able to find new opportunities and build on them quickly because you do not have to go through the school of hard knocks. You can accomplish this by having experienced people mentoring you. The best mentor is someone who has already achieved what you

# Chapter 17

## The First Season
*Solving People's Problems – Even on Television*

- **Love Us or Hate Us**
- **Ratings Skyrocket**
- **Shouting from the Back Room**
- **A Regular Guy**
- **Business Heats Up**
- **Stress Builds**
- **Rancho Montelongo**
- **Another TV Contract**

### Love Us or Hate Us

People loved the show. The day after the show premiered, we got hundreds of phone calls and e-mails congratulating us. Others wrote e-mails to the network saying how much we rocked.

But not everybody loved us. Some local investors were critical of what we did. A magazine in Houston wrote a story quoting some investors who slammed us. Later, I found out those investors had allegedly auditioned for the same show, so maybe it was sour grapes.

want to do. Sometimes, just listening to a mentor's whisper is enough to spur you to success.

This is why I am so passionate about mentoring you. I know that in order to sustain success, you will need sustained guidance. When you have sustained guidance, you can compound your business growth very quickly because you have a treasure of experience to draw on. As you achieve success, I know I have done my job.

This is when you start to build wealth. This is when business becomes fun.

The previous cast had done several shows, and had a viewership that was considered relatively healthy. When our show aired, some of the old fans e-mailed in: "Bring back the old team!" "This new guy won't last long!" "He's mean!" "He doesn't treat subcontractors right!"

## Ratings Skyrocket

During the second episode, we went crazy. We decided to have a competition to see who could make more profit flipping a house. It was my brother and me against Veronica and my sister-in-law.

Veronica and my sister-in-law stole my contractors. They bought them lunch and had them work on their flip jobsite. I decided to fight fire with fire. I got a bunch of bikini girls and alcohol, and I stole my contractors back. At one point, one of my contractors was on Veronica's job site eating ice cream. I grabbed the ice cream cone and threw it against the wall.

That really upset viewers. A&E's Web site message board was inundated. People wrote stuff like: "They're nasty!" "Armando's mean!" "He's an asshole!" "We hate Armando!" "We hate those guys!"

My family was feeling the heat, too. Our relatives said, "What are you doing? Are you crazy?! You're going to ruin our family name!"

But I said, "We are on the right track. This is what we've always done. It's an evolutionary process. Those people who hate us now are going to be our most loyal fans."

When criticism persisted, I said, "You think I'm gonna turn it down? I'm just getting started. We're gonna turn it up!"

# Chapter Q

## How to Save on Taxes
Earn a Bundle by Understanding Legal Structures

- **Your Rights**
- **Flip Your Own House**
- **How to Live in Your House for Free**
- **More Savings**
- **Another Way to Save on Taxes**
- **Legal Entities**
- **Write Off Vacations**

### Your Rights

We live in a phenomenal country and America would not be what it is without taxes. At the same time, it's your American duty and right to minimize your taxes. You want to keep as much money as possible in your pocket, while still paying rightful taxes on net profit.

As an individual, you could have capital gains taxes from flipping houses. You will typically incur a larger tax base as an individual than you will as a corporation. As a business person, you will have taxes on your legal entities. One strategy is to run your flips through a corporation as a way to lower your tax base.

The ratings took off, jumping from about 800,000 viewers for my first episode to a range of 1.1 million to 1.4 million viewers for the third episode. That is equivalent to 11 to 14 college football stadiums of fans per episode. On top of that, the ratings actually maintained their high numbers for repeat shows, which is unusual in an industry where ratings typically drop for reruns.

Each of our episodes typically ran two to six times a week, for three to four weeks, with each season's shows repeated several times throughout the year. At an average 1.1 million viewers per episode with reruns, roughly 36 million people would see us after just a few episodes.

We were building a huge, loyal fan base. We were taking the show to a whole new level!

Something magical happened after our third episode. It was called "Intern Affairs." I was interviewing interns who wanted to learn the real estate business. An intern named Chris stated his desire to make money, but did not have any belief in his own abilities.

I grabbed one of my most prized possessions off my office wall. It was a framed application for food-stamp assistance that I had filled out in California. I explained to Chris that at the time, Veronica and I were living on food stamps and were $50,000 in debt.

It was not my original intention to tell the entire country on TV how we had once been on the brink of financial disaster. In the show's introduction, we already mentioned that we had driven into town on our last tank of gas. I never planned to tell people all the details of how we got there.

However, that one episode changed the course of the entire show and ultimately, our lives. We were flooded by tens of thousands of e-mails from people who felt moved by the fact that Veronica and I had once

See your CPA to determine what strategies will work best in your situation. How do you tell a good CPA from a bad one? Bad CPAs talk a lot about avoiding red flags with the IRS. These guys are terrified, broke or do not have wealthy clients. Good CPAs talk about ways to prevent the IRS from overcharging so you can keep massive amounts of profits in your pocket.

### Flip Your Own House

You can make money by flipping the house you live in. If you use no other techniques from this book, just this one strategy can save you tens of thousands of dollars.

If you are going to be in the market for real estate, you may as well buy your personal residence at a discount and make profits. One great way to do this is to buy an undervalued property, fix it up, live in it for two years and sell it.

If you lived in it for at least two out of the last five years, you do not have to pay capital gains taxes – on profits up to $250,000 if you are single, and up to $500,000 if you are married. This is an incredible way to build wealth and essentially live in a house for free.

Let me give you some numbers. Suppose we take a house that has an after-repair value of $500,000. If you use the 70 Percent Rule, you would get a loan of $350,000 from hard-money lenders.

I'm going to break down these numbers further. The hard-money loan includes the cost of repairs and closing. The total loan amount of $350,000 is based on a purchase price of

lived on food stamps. It inspired viewers to believe that they could flip houses, too.

People realized that I had a purpose and a larger "why" for my sense of urgency for myself and others who worked for me. This is when viewers really got behind us and helped make "Flip This House" a hit reality show.

With all the reruns, by our fourth episode in October 2006, we had between 40 million and 60 million viewers of the show.

Now, the e-mails raved about us. They said things like: "Armando is a genius!" "That guy rocks!" "You're my hero!" "Armando is my inspiration." "You make me believe in myself when no one else has."

Over the next few shows, we let viewers into our lives more, and I let viewers see some of my mistakes, such as when I went over budget, fired contractors who stole from me, faced unexpected problems and personality conflicts or dealt with other challenges. I realized how powerful it was for people to learn from my mistakes. I wanted people to see it's a fun business, but also give viewers the reality side of it.

The flips we featured on the show were the hardest ones in our inventory. That's because they are more dramatic for television and give people the opportunity to learn more. But most of the houses we flip each month are pretty routine because I have my system in place already.

### Shouting from the Back Room

You would think that homeowners would love being on TV and negotiating with us to buy their house. Not so. Off camera, people are willing to sell their house at a dirt-cheap price, but they don't

$300,000, plus $40,000 in repair costs and $10,000 in lending fees and closing costs. So the total loan is $350,000.

You use the repair money to fix up the house. A hard-money lender gives you the money to do this; a conventional bank will not. But once the house is fixed, the conventional lender will lend on it. After six months, the hard-money loan is "seasoned" and you can refinance the loan into a "rate-and-term" mortgage.

Let's say you get a 30-year fixed loan at 7 percent interest. You would then have a monthly payment – including principal and interest, but excluding taxes and insurance – of $2,328. You can go to any mortgage calculator Web site to figure out how much the monthly payments on a loan will be. In this case, I have rounded the numbers to keep it simple.

At the end of two years, you will have paid approximately $48,000 in interest, which is tax deductible. In the meantime, you have been making monthly payments of $2,328. Multiplied by 24 months, that's about $56,000 for two years. Well, $48,000 of that is tax deductible.

Let's say your job pays $80,000 a year. Normally, you would have to pay federal and state income taxes on that. But when you subtract the tax deduction of $24,000 per year, that leaves a taxable income of $56,000.

Instead of paying 30 percent tax on $80,000 income, you're paying 30 percent on $56,000. Rather than paying $24,000 in taxes, you're paying $16,800 in taxes. That's a difference of $7,200.

There's more. Let's say the market increases 8 percent each year.

want the world to know that they've sold it for so little. This makes negotiation much more difficult.

With the TV show, I still did everything as I had always done, except now I would be walking into people's homes with a cameraman filming everything. But I simply let homeowners know: "Just because the TV crew is here and the cameras are on, it doesn't change that you have a need. You need to sell this house."

Most of the homeowners I talk to are having problems. And I solve problems. Ultimately, people are grateful that we got them out of a bad situation.

One deal took some work to get around this challenge. Two sisters, Mary Lou and Josephine, inherited their house from their mother after she died. Their mother had not paid the taxes for four years, and the tax collector would be foreclosing in three weeks.

They had seen me in a TV interview and called. When I got there, cameraman in tow, Mary Lou opened the door. She said that her younger sister Josephine did not want to be on camera.

"Well, tell your sister she doesn't have to be in the room," I said. "I'll be there, the camera will be there, but she doesn't have to show her face."

Mary Lou let me in and I sat in the living room listening to her while Josephine shouted from the bedroom.

I listened to their story, as I have always done. I had told the camera people that this might take awhile, because I have got to find out what the problem is that the person needs solved.

After the first year, the house will be worth $540,000, after the second year $583,200 and in the third year $630,000.

You had $150,000 in equity when you bought the property. When you add appreciation of $83,000 gained after two years, the house has total equity of $230,000.

This means you could make $200,000 in profit when you sell the house. After subtracting two years of approximately $56,000 in payments, you have a total profit of about $150,000. So you have lived in your house for free for two years, plus made a profit.

That's a great way to build wealth, just by flipping your own residence.

### How to Live in Your House for Free

The next page has an example of how to live in your house for free. Just follow the numbers. We'll use round numbers for simplicity.

In the end, Mary Lou was willing to sell me the house. But Josephine did not want to sell.

"I know you! I've seen you on TV!" boomed Josephine's voice from the back room. "I know you make a lot of money! We don't have to sell this house any cheaper than what we're asking for it!"

"Look," I said. "I negotiate on TV not for the fun of negotiating, but because the numbers have to work. This has to work for you first. Then it has to work for me. If it doesn't work for you, then we don't make a deal."

Silence.

"I don't want to seem like a sucker on TV," said Josephine.

"Why don't you come out of the room?" I asked. "I don't like talking through walls. But before you come out, why don't you tell me what it is that you really need."

"Well," she said. "I don't want my mom's house to be foreclosed on. But I need $3,000 to move. I want to take all my stuff with me."

"If I can solve your problem, and I give you $3,000 to help you move, will you let me buy the house at the price I need?" I asked.

She paused for a moment, and then said, "Yes."

Josephine finally came out of the bedroom and talked to me in person. She had long brown hair, a wrinkled face, sad eyes, teeth that were gray from smoking, and horn-rimmed glasses.

The sisters still did not want to be filmed, and I respected that. I asked the crew to turn the camera off while I finished negotiating with them. I kept my word to them and the house never appeared on the show.

| | |
|---|---|
| $500,000 | After-Repair Value |
| $300,000 | Purchase price |
| $ 40,000 | Repairs |
| $ 10,000 | Lender fees and closing costs |
| ---------- | |
| $350,000 | Total loan amount |
| 7% | Interest rate on 30-year fixed loan |
| $ 2328 | Monthly payment |
| x 24 | months |
| ---------- | |
| $ 55,872 | Total payments in two years |
| $ 20,000 | Property taxes and insurance paid |
| $150,000 | Equity upon purchase |
| $ 83,200 | Appreciation after two years, based on 8 percent per year |
| ---------- | |
| $233,200 | Total equity after two years |
| - $ 75,872 | Total mortgage payments (principal, interest, taxes and insurance) |
| ---------- | |
| $157,328 | Profit |

**More Savings**

This does not include the fact that over two years you have paid down the principal balance of your home. If your principal and interest payment was $2,328 at 7 percent interest on a 30-year-

**A Regular Guy**

With a camera crew, I sometimes had to work harder at being a regular guy with homeowners.

This happened with one house we were filming. That day, I was driving a nice car. I usually drive a less flashy car when buying a house. But that day, I drove my shiny, blue Mercedes CLS 500. I wore shorts, flip-flops and a hat.

As I walked up to the seller's house, loud music was blasting and I saw the homeowner holding a beer. With my car and outfit, I was afraid he would think that I was someone with a lot of money who just wanted to take him to the cleaners. I needed to somehow make this man realize I was a regular guy.

"Hey, you got another beer?" I asked.

We sat on his patio drinking beer. And we talked.

"I'm just like you," I said. "I'm a regular guy. I went through a foreclosure before, just like you. Now you need to sell your house. I've been there. I've been down in the dumps. I'm just like you."

We did the deal.

**Business Heats Up**

Our business was heating up. We were getting all kinds of leads from people who saw the show. People called from all over the country. They wanted me to buy their mother's house or their commercial property. Construction workers called from all over the country wanting to work with us.

fixed mortgage, you would have paid down approximately $7,367 of principal. You can add this to your total equity after two years which goes to your bottom line and brings your total to $164,695.

The tax benefits give you even more savings. Since the federal government allows you to deduct the mortgage interest and the property taxes on your home, you can add this into your bottom line. At the same interest scenario above, you have paid out $48,517 in interest and approximately $14,000 in property taxes. This means you have $62,517 in expenses that you can subtract from your yearly taxes. Now, this $62,517 decreases your tax base, and at a 30 percent tax rate, it would save you approximately $18,755 over two years!

Add this to your bottom line and in two years you have put $183,450 in total profit in your pocket with no hard work involved. This is the beauty of real estate. Forget living for free. You were paid more than $90,000 per year just to live in your home. That is what flipping and growing rich is all about!

|  |  |
|---|---|
| $157,328 | Profit |
| + 7,367 | Equity from mortgage principal |
| ---------- | |
| $164,695 | |
| + 18,755 | Tax savings |
| ---------- | |
| $183,450 | Total profit |

## Another Way to Save on Taxes

Here's another way to save on taxes. Use the profit that you made from the sale of one house as a down payment to buy the next house.

A former NBA player who saw us on TV even called to say he needed help. "Can you get me out of foreclosure?" he asked. We signed a contract.

By mid-2006, the business was flipping about 30 houses a month. Our first episode was on July 23rd of 2006, so the vast majority of our leads came from the systems that I had put in place for finding great deals.

I was also getting thousands of e-mails from fans. "How did you get started flipping houses?" "How did you go from $50,000 in debt to making that much?" "How can I start flipping with no credit?"

I realized that I had a message people wanted to hear. There are a lot of people who are in the situation I used to be in. I decided I need to tell them how to flip houses.

**Stress Builds**

The show started to affect our personal lives. When we walked down the street, people would congratulate us. "You make San Antonio look good!" they said. "You make real estate investors look good!"

When we went on vacation, I realized the vast popularity of our show. People stopped us everywhere. From people rushing to take our picture in New York's Chinatown to fans in Acapulco, Mexico wanting autographs, Veronica and I knew the tide had turned.

By summer 2006, we started to feel the stress. We were flipping 30 houses a month and filming three to five shows at a time getting ready for our first season on TV. Meanwhile, Veronica and I had sold our own house and moved to a hotel while we waited to close and fix up our new ranch home.

When you sell the old house, you will not get taxed as long as profits are less than $500,000 for couples or $250,000 for singles. This applies if you have lived in the house for two of the last five years.

When you buy your next house, you can keep your monthly payments low by using the profit from the first house as down payment for the new house.

Even if the price of the next house is higher, your loan amount may be the same as your previous house because of the large down payment, so your monthly payment stays the same.

If you move every two years and roll the profits, you can keep buying bigger houses but keep the same low monthly payment.

This strategy helps you increase your lifestyle while you save on taxes. You are combining a tax strategy the IRS already gives you – by living in your primary residence for two years then selling and not having to pay taxes on the profits – with the power of flipping houses.

In short, this method:

1. Explodes your equity in your primary residence.

2. Allows you to increase your lifestyle.

3. Reduces or eliminates taxes on your profits of the sale of your home.

4. Keeps your monthly payments at about the same amount as your last residence.

We were letting people see our personal lives more on the show. I didn't mind letting the camera get in our faces, but sometimes it was a strain. I learned to tell the cameramen to stop. If I didn't want something to be shot about me, I asked them to stop filming. I learned to turn the microphone off.

With all this happening, flipping houses was the least amount of stress. I had a great system for flipping by now, and the business had been running smoothly for a long time. If I had not had my business system down, all the other stuff would have been impossible to do.

## Rancho Montelongo

Veronica and I moved into our new ranch home in June 2006. We called it Rancho Montelongo.

It was a 4,500-square-foot house on 3 acres in a prime part of town. The house had five bedrooms and four baths. The entire upstairs was a 1,500-square-foot master suite. The property had a swimming pool, chicken coop, three horse stables and 70 species of trees.

Of course, I got it for a steal.

A gentleman who knew the property owner had called me. To this day, I do not know why the owner wanted to sell it. But when I finally talked to him, he said, "Make me an offer." That's usually a sign that someone is willing to negotiate.

This was an unusual situation because it was one of the few times I did not actually know the owner's problem. He seemed to just want to make a deal and get rid of it.

### Legal Entities

You can also save on taxes through the legal entity you set up to do business. Different entities serve different investment purposes.

The legal entity that I use for flipping houses is a C-Corp. The U.S. government gives us more than 400 legal tax deductions by using a C-Corp. So when I am flipping for big profits, I use a C-Corp to keep my tax base low. This is one reason why the rich get richer.

I do not put my personal residence in a corporation since Texas has strong homestead laws, which protect my primary residence. Check with your lawyer about protecting your personal residence.

### Write Off Vacations

As a real estate investor, you can write off all your vacations if you look at real estate opportunities while on your trip.

When I go on vacation, I always go as a business trip, as president of one of my corporations. It does not matter where we go, because I know how to flip houses and buy real estate in any market. There's always an opportunity to do business.

During my trips, I always make sure to honestly look at one or two real estate deals, collect information about a property and pick up a name card from a real estate agent. I write down the property address and attach the information so there's proof that I looked at a property.

The property was worth $650,000 fixed up. But it was a 1970s house and needed a lot of updating. I offered $220,000. The owner took it. I was pleasantly surprised.

We dropped $115,000 in repairs and upgrades. I created the new floor plan, and Veronica designed the look. We put in travertine floors; stainless steel appliances; custom cabinets; walk-in closets; dual-person showers; a Roman Jacuzzi tub; and customized wood cabinetry, with places for cufflinks and sunglasses.

We sold our old house within 16 days. We used the profits from that sale as down payment on our new house. Because we had lived in the last house for more than two years and rolled the equity into this one, the tax collector did not take anything. This meant that our monthly payments on the new house were about the same as they were at the last house.

We were able to improve our lifestyle without increasing our bills.

Moving into this house was a rich, satisfying reward. But the house itself was not that important to me. What really made it a dream home was that Mondo Man, Veronica and I lived here as a family.

One of my favorite things about this property was swimming in the pool with my son at night. Because of all the trees, we couldn't see any of our neighbors. When we looked up into the sky, all we saw were stars.

## Another TV Contract

The first season of our TV show ended in November 2006. By then, we had done six shows. We were the highest-rated cast for "Flip This House," and we were the highest-rated flip show on all the TV channels.

When traveling with your family members, you can also write off their expenses if they are employees of your corporation.

With our family, I write off Veronica's expenses because she's part of my corporation. I am also able to write off Mondo Man's expenses because he's a part of my TV show's marketing. You may or may not be able to do this with your children, but if you hire them in some way, you can write off their expenses.

Of course, whether you file taxes as an individual or corporation, see a good real estate attorney and CPA.

We also were the only cast to be asked to do another season of "Flip This House." Our ratings were so phenomenal that the producers decided to take on other casts in other parts of the country. The others did not do as well as our show in the ratings, but they still pulled in viewers.

A&E asked us to do another season. We signed a contract for a second season of 10 episodes, which started March 2007.

# Chapter R

## Other Investments
Building Long-Term Wealth

- **Business Partners**
- **Focus**
- **Downside of Wealth**
- **Now Cash vs. Future Cash**
- **Rental and Commercial Properties**
- **International Markets**
- **Larger Benefits**

### Business Partners

Donald Trump said that if not for a prenuptial agreement, his divorce would have buried him in the late 1980s.

A business divorce can also bury you. You are not necessarily going to have a prenup agreement for your business partner, but if you do take on partners, here's what I recommend:

- Take on business partners only on a deal-by-deal basis.
- Use partners for money, credit or to acquire properties.
- Never give anyone authority over your money.

# Chapter 18

## The Second Season
### *Expanding My Business Scope*

- **Highest Ratings**
- **Remembering My Promise**
- **The Cat House**
- **A Family Split**
- **Veronica's Deal**
- **Veronica's Promotion**
- **Rentals and Commercial Deals**
- **Flipping in Other Markets**
- **New Mentors**
- **City Benefits**

### Highest Ratings

The second season of our "Flip This House" show started filming in November 2006.

It was a huge hit. Millions of viewers followed the show. Tens of thousands of fans wrote e-mails asking questions about the show. We had hundreds of people attending our seminars. Other channels copied our show, with rehabbers wearing dark sunglasses like we did. Comedians even spoofed our show.

- Make decisions on a financial basis first.
- Make sure you, your partner and partner's spouse share the same goals.

People ask me, "Should I have a partner in business?" And my answer is, "Should you get married?" Both require a commitment.

No one really knows what a partner is going to be like until you hit tough times and you disagree. You have to create assurances that you are both going to be solvent and liquid.

Use money or credit partners, but only on a deal-by-deal basis. It's easy enough to get out of one deal if you have to, but it is much more difficult to get out of 100 deals with a partner.

Make sure that you and your partner share the same goals and work ethics. Early in my career, I had a partner whose wife would call him at 6 p.m., and he would leave the office while I worked until late at night. When you take on a partner, you are also taking on the spouse. Make sure you all have the same goals.

It is often said that behind every good man is a great woman. I genuinely believe that. In fact, it is one of the few clichés I believe. Many men are too focused on looking for good women to get focused on making money. It isn't until they meet that great one that their life changes.

I also believe the opposite of that is true. If you have a business partner who does not have a great partner behind him or her, this can be detrimental to your business. When you choose business partners, make sure their spouses' beliefs are aligned with yours.

We got great exposure from the media. Entertainment Weekly called the show, "Real estate at its dramatic best… San Antonio's mega-macho Armando Montelongo is still the guy we love to hate." The San Antonio Express-News referred to us as "the colorful, audacious and, to some viewers anyway, offensive Montelongos."

In terms of deals, I was America's biggest and most notorious flipper.

## Remembering My Promise

When my TV show started, I thought it would entertain people. I had no idea that the show would touch people's lives and inspire them.

From our very first episode, even though a few people didn't like the show, I got thousands of e-mails asking how to flip houses. People said, "Teach me how to do it. Help me, coach me and teach me. Show me how you do it."

The mail was so high that it reminded me of the promise I made – to share the keys I hold to success.

## The Cat House

In January 2007, while filming the second season's shows that would start airing in March, I came across the hardest flip of my life.

I couldn't sleep for days because I was so worried about this house. I went over budget twice. I split with my brother after this deal. Veronica sent me to see a psychotherapist. I wondered if I had finally met my match.

I called this "The Cat House." The TV producers called it the "The Little House of Horrors."

If you go into business with family, the same rules apply. Make sure your ultimate goals, dreams and work ethics are aligned. If you are married to your business partner, make sure you define clear roles and boundaries in your business and marriage.

In my business, I am the president and my wife is vice-president, so I have final say. She trusts my decisions based on my experience. But in our marriage, we are equal partners and consult each other on problems and decisions.

**Focus**

Remember: you are in the business of helping people.

In my opinion, you have a moral obligation as a flipper. If you promise to help people and you deliberately let their houses go into foreclosure without making efforts to help them or pass those properties to other investors who can help, it's ethically wrong. It's also business suicide. You lose referrals and deals, because you have no credibility.

I always put my real estate business first, because that's what created my wealth. Even though I do public speaking and training workshops, I take care of my real estate first.

Whether you invest in real estate on a part-time or full-time basis, you still have to maintain a level of focus. Focus does not mean working hard. It means working smart.

Don't just focus on getting rich for yourself. Focus on helping people.

Three other investors had previously turned down buying, fixing and flipping this house. But I bought it.

The original homeowner was paranoid about people seeing the house. She would talk to me calmly one day and the next day accuse me of vandalizing and stealing things from the house, even though I did not have the keys.

I could not get inside, so I walked around the house and peeked through the windows. It was trashed. But I didn't know how bad it really was until after I bought it and went inside.

I rarely buy a house without seeing the inside, but the numbers were so good on this one that I didn't think it would be a problem. I don't recommend anyone ever doing that unless they are very experienced rehabbers.

Once I was inside, I found that it was 4 feet deep in trash. It was covered with discarded boxes, clothes, toys, newspapers, hamburger boxes, cans and cat poop. The smell was nauseating. The neighbors could smell it five houses down.

The former owners had raised 15 cats there. There were still stray cats, rats, mice and roaches running around. Later, we found the bodies of two dead dogs and the skeleton of a cat's head. The cats were eating the rats, the rats were eating the kittens, the kittens were eating the roaches and the roaches were eating the cat poop. The whole place was its own ecosystem.

The bathroom was filled 2 feet high with opened cat food cans. Above the toilet was a fly strip with hundreds of stuck flies. The bathroom was so packed I could not fully open the door.

I called my contractor in to clear out the house. He went in and immediately came out. "I won't do it," he said. "It's too disgusting."

**Downside of Wealth**

I can't say a single bad thing about being rich and having money. But sometimes you might encounter controversy.

Because of my celebrity position now, people sometimes threaten to call the media or sue me for things that don't make sense, as a way to extort money. But I am a businessman, and I do not fold to false claims or threats. I believe that as long as you are honest and have integrity, you will be vindicated. I would rather be vindicated in a court of law than cave in to false threats. In some ways, controversy comes with fame.

But you don't have to be like me. The great thing about real estate is that you can be a loud or quiet millionaire. Whether you are introverted or extroverted, tough or soft, the most important thing is to stay true and honest.

**Now Cash vs. Future Cash**

Real estate is like a game of Monopoly. You acquire property after property and build house after house.

But instead of starting with small rental houses, you want to start your real estate business by flipping houses, move to rental houses, then to commercial buildings. As you build your cash reserves, you win the game of Monopoly and your life.

You have "now" cash and "future" cash. "Now" cash is your flipping money. "Future" cash is your residual rental money.

As you flip more houses, you generate more now cash. Setting aside now cash helps build your cash reserves. You then use this

I asked two more contractors to clean it. They also refused.

I called a company that specialized in hazardous waste material. I had budgeted $3,000 to clear out the house. This company agreed to do it but charged nearly $14,000.

It took eight 40-yard trash bins to remove the garbage from the house. It took a week and a half to clear out enough trash so that our feet could touch the floor.

Since the trash was nearly 4 feet high, the cats had urinated that high. The contractor cut out the walls 4 feet around the house, leaving just the bare wood studs.

We sprayed the entire house with anti-bacterial solution. Then we went back and bleached everything. Next, we wiped down every square inch of the property with anti-bacterial solution. After that, we used special anti-bacterial and deodorizing paint to seal in any smell. We scraped all the insulation out of the attic. Then we put in new insulation and drywall.

After all that, there was still a lingering smell, and I couldn't figure out what it was. It turned out to be the sewage pipe. The pipes had cracked under the house because tree roots had grown and clogged the sewage.

The plumber found the sewage breaks by using a line with a camera. That alone cost $200. But what really cost money was digging a tunnel underneath the house to get to the pipes and fix them. That cost $24,000.

Normally, I find problems in a house before buying it, like if a sewage pipe is broken. But this time, I missed it because of all the trash and the odor from the cats.

Then, my roofer Randy found leaks, which could cause mold. We fixed the leaks and cleared that there was no mold.

## SPENDING "NOW" CASH TO INVEST AND BUILD "FUTURE" CASH LEADS TO TRUE WEALTH

to buy rental and commercial properties. Rental and commercial properties generate residual income – money over time. This is your long-term wealth, your future cash.

Next, combine your now cash and residual income to create profit regeneration. Profit regeneration is reinvesting your profits to create a larger source of long-term income, which

This house had been one disaster after another, costing me more money than I had expected. I lost many nights of sleep.

Veronica was so worried she had me see a psychotherapist. I did not want to go, but I said I would because of her. I talked to the psychotherapist for an hour. She pointed out that my brother and I had been having tension because of differences in how we do business, and this house had cracked everything wide open, creating a lot of stress.

I thought the whole session was pretty useless, and I told Veronica that. I knew that ultimately, if I were going to be successful, it would be up to me. There was no way I would let one house beat me. I decided, "Armando is back!"

In the end, the house got new bathrooms, kitchen cabinets, sinks, counters, insulation, sewage, plumbing, walls, paint and trim. It was beautiful. The 2,000-square-foot house was like brand-new.

When it was done, the neighbors thanked us. The city officials congratulated us for solving a problem they had dealt with for six years.

My equity in the house was about $25,000. When I finally walked away, I pounded my chest and shouted, "I beat you, Cat House!"

It is now one of my most coveted properties and definitely my most enjoyable transformation ever! To be honest, the average investor would have lost a fortune on this property. However, because of my experience, I was able to turn lemons into big profits!

## A Family Split

It was hard to split with my brother. Although we are close as a family, we had different business philosophies and visions for the future.

means your money works for you. When you properly reinvest your money, this money will make more money for you than you can by working for an employer. This is the essence of profit regeneration.

So you use your profits to invest in more long-term income, which means your money works for you. This creates more profit regeneration.

When you have now cash, residual income and profit generation working together, then and only then should you spend your money on luxury items such as cars, homes on the beach and yachts.

## Rental and Commercial Properties

Flipping houses gives you the cash to start. You do not have to buy rental or commercial properties until later. These types of investments require cash. They generate cash flow and wealth over the long term, but you also need cash to get them going.

Here's one rule of thumb:

Only take on as many rental properties as you can afford the missed payments. If the rental property mortgage is $1,000, and your tenants move out, can you comfortably afford the $1,000 payment?

The problem is that people get stuck on the idea of finding great deals for rentals. They buy two or three good deals, and all of a sudden they have $3,000 in payments. They find several tenants, but if the tenants all move out, they have $3,000 of debt each month.

So we decided to go our separate ways. It was like going through a business divorce, and it was one of the toughest times of my life. At the time of the split, we had between 75 to 100 flips, and it took 10 months to settle everything.

The split was tough emotionally. Because my brother and I were very close and because there were millions of dollars at stake, it was a stressful time. I decided not to fight over properties, but keep family relationships ahead of making money.

We agreed to split the properties 50-50. He kept the properties he had analyzed and purchased for the company, and I kept the properties I had analyzed and purchased.

Whenever you take a company and rip it in two, it can be financially tough, and it was. However, I say with the utmost pride because of the effort that it took, that I paid all of my mortgages and still have great relationships with these private investors and hard-money lenders.

Because I had spent the previous years creating cash reserves and regenerating profit, I was able to finance all my properties in the split. If I had not followed my own principles that I now teach, it might have taken me down.

I had been flipping houses before I brought my brother into the business, so I knew it was not necessary to have partners. Ultimately, you do not need a business partner to flip houses.

This may sound strange, but after our split, my brother actually let many of his houses go into foreclosure. These were houses he had acquired and kept – as many as 27 houses with up to $1.5 million in equity. They were great deals, with lots of potential profit.

But he started going into other businesses which, in my opinion, diverted his attention. It's not that he was in a financial bind and

If you want to go from a having a great life and saving money to having a great life that works, you don't want to be a slave to rental properties. Rental properties are great, but have the capital reserves so that you always feel that rental properties are great.

If you have a commercial property with a $10,000 monthly mortgage, and two of your tenants move out, can you afford to be short $2,000 a month in rent? Make sure you have enough cash reserves to cover that $2,000 while those units sit vacant.

Down the road, I'll teach students how to own rental properties without stressing out. You do it by building five years' worth of reserves. Flipping properties is a way to create cash reserves first.

When you are ready to buy rental and commercial properties, you can use the same principles and techniques as when you are flipping properties.

As you are flipping houses, hone your skills so you will be ready to buy rental and commercial properties. Hone your skills for buying, negotiating, selling and managing so that you can immediately start generating cash flow.

You want to hone your skills so you can become a great landlord down the road. A lot of people who become landlords do not actually have the skills to do that. They have properties that sit vacant. They don't know how to fix problems. They let contractors take advantage of them. They end up with negative cash flow.

Never buy a rental property at full market value. When you

could not afford the payments. It seemed to me that he just did not focus on his real estate business. After too many missed payments, the lenders foreclosed on the houses.

## Veronica's Deal

Meanwhile, Veronica was coming into her own as a flipper. Up to now, she had focused on sales and design – at which she is amazing. Now she was taking on more.

One deal in particular she earned her stripes. I had purchased a house for $55,000. The property needed about $12,000 in repairs, and when it was done, it would be worth $110,000. This meant the property cost about 55 cents on the dollar with repairs.

I handed the deal over to Veronica. She went in and looked through the property. I gave her a tight budget of $12,000 for repairs.

The house had some shift in the foundation. Veronica had an engineer look at it, who said it was good enough to sell. The foundation had settled but did not need to be fixed.

But the house was old and dirty. The kitchen needed refurbishing and the carpets needed replacing. The previous owners had kids who left dirty fingerprint on the walls.

To save money on replacing the kitchen cabinets, Veronica hired a trim carpenter to build some new cabinets. She had him stain the new cabinets to match the rest. The old and new cabinets looked perfectly alike.

Veronica then saved money on the kitchen countertop. Instead of replacing the entire countertop, which cost $1,200, she found out about a spray that cost $350. The special spray makes an old, plastic laminate countertop look brand-new.

buy undervalue, you will be able to generate positive cash flow. You want to use the same techniques you used to buy houses for flipping:

- The 70 Percent Rule
- No-money-down methods
- Leveraging other people's money

Build cash reserves and practice profit regeneration to keep your rental properties profitable.

Do the same with commercial properties. Always buy them undervalue so you can walk in with little or no money down. If you are going to buy a commercial building to flip, it will typically need repair. But you can fix it up and still create positive cash flow.

All the skills you honed while buying residential properties will come into play when buying rental and commercial properties. You will use your skills for buying, repairing, negotiating and managing properties. The beauty is that you will be generating great income as you sharpen your skills, so you will be paid to learn.

As you play Monopoly in real life, you will be able to win with rental and commercial properties.

### International Markets

The principles of real estate investing and flipping can be used all over the world. No matter what country you're in, you can use the same formulas because they are a prudent way of making money anywhere.

When she was done, she had spent only $7,000 of the $12,000 budget.

That's when I realized she was on her way. She had learned enough. It was time to move her up in the business, promote her and give her a big project.

Through years of dedication, she had done a fantastic job. She now had a sense of satisfaction coming in under budget and the confidence to do more flips.

## Veronica's Promotion

I promoted Veronica to vice president. She had honed her skills as a saleswoman and started doing her own flips, too. This was a great asset to our business as well as a source of strength for our family.

Veronica was a phenomenal saleswoman. She was able to sell as many as 24 houses in a month. She was particularly good at owner-financed properties. People trusted her. She is not a licensed real estate agent, but you do not need a license if you are selling your own property.

I made the mistake of thinking that because Veronica is my wife, she would work for free. She said no.

"I need to have a value, and I need to feel like I'm getting paid," she said.

So I gave her a healthy salary. Then she asked to earn commission on her sales to give her motivation. I agreed to that, as well. And she did very well.

She was still a mom. She took Mondo Man to school, worked from 9 a.m. to 3 p.m., picked him up from school, took him home and continued her work as a mom the rest of the day. Because we had systems in place,

These principles are based upon a universal language, which is known to all of us. It's called math. Numbers. One plus one always equals two. Seventy percent of any property value is always a good deal and 50 percent is always a heck of a deal.

Never pay 100 percent for a property. Start with the 70 Percent Rule and build from there. Find a motivated seller, get the deal and money will follow. Then look for a buyer.

When I'm prospecting properties around the world, I use these same principles. No matter what country you're in, this is how you build your flipping business. If you buy overseas, this is how you build your international real estate business.

Democratic markets are opening up all over the world. These real estate investing principles can be used throughout these markets.

### Larger Benefits

Regardless of where you are, you can help people by investing in real estate. As you begin flipping houses, you will have homeowners thanking you for buying their property when they were in distress.

When you flip houses, the rewards you receive are often more than just financial. You are helping a distressed homeowner get out of a situation or giving a homebuyer their dream home. You are helping to improve a neighborhood, community, local economy and city.

everything got done. She worked as much or as little as she wanted. She was able to work, as well as fulfill her needs as a wife and mother.

It was a relief for me, too. I knew I would never have to worry about Veronica's future. If anything bad ever happened to me, I knew Veronica could take care of herself and our son.

When we're at home, it's different from when we're at the office. The dynamics are different, yet we have found a happy balance between the two.

When I'm at home, I'm Veronica's husband and she's my wife. We have an equal partnership. We have marriage and family goals, not work goals. We have a love life.

When we're at work, I am the leader. I have more experience with the business. I have to run the company with speed and good judgment. I told Veronica that I would not consult her on my business decisions because I never did before she joined the company.

She said, "Well, you know the business. I don't." However, she has learned the business.

Once I had a contractor who wanted to get paid, and I did not pay him because he didn't do enough work. Veronica questioned me about it. She's not as rough around the edges as I am.

So I let her do it her way. She decided to pay the contractor out of guilt, rather than based on his work. Well, he walked off on her. She lost the money. So she learned her lesson through the school of hard knocks. She thought she knew better, but she got burned.

"OK, we'll do it your way," she said after that.

But she has earned her stripes. People can see me coming a mile away on sales, but they never see her coming.

# Chapter S

## How You Can Start Flipping
Create a New Future

- **Find a Mentor**
- **Learn from the Best**
- **Proven Systems**
- **Serve Yourself**
- **Share the Knowledge**
- **Change Your Future**
- **How You Can Learn**

### Find a Mentor

In this book you've caught a glimpse of my world, of how I went from being very broke to very rich. You've seen my trials, tribulations and triumphs.

Your success will depend on how you manage your flipping business, whether you're new at it or you're experienced and would like to double your business. Either way, you want to find more successful people to take you to the next level.

Being an entrepreneur, I am somewhat of a free spirit. I will listen to people at first. But once I get the hang of it, I'll take off on my own before I've learned enough.

## Rental and Commercial Deals

By now, I had built up enough cash reserves to diversify into other types of real estate, such as rental and commercial buildings. These would help me create long-term wealth.

I started looking at condominiums all along the Texas coastline because the market has been hot. Those condos rent out very easily, and appreciation has been nearly 20 percent a year. It's a fast way to build wealth.

The condos were priced between $200,000 and $400,000 each. With the package deal, I would get them at a 20 percent to 25 percent discount. If the market grows 18 percent in one year, I would have a 43 percent increase.

At the time of this writing, I am negotiating to pick up the majority share of the complex.

I also picked up a 6,000-square-foot commercial building. That's not a large building, but it was a great deal. The building was worth $375,000. I bought it for $115,000, which was the amount of the owner's mortgage.

I picked up this property from a gentleman with financial troubles, who needed to sell everything he owned. I applied for a bank loan to buy the building.

The bank saw that the building had $260,000 equity. They ran my credit, which was now excellent. The bank wrote me a loan requiring no money down. The property had huge equity, so there was little risk to the bank.

On a commercial property, the bank normally wants you to put between 15 percent and 30 percent down. But I explained to

But I've paid heavily for it. As I mentioned, I lost $60,000 on one deal because I was not willing to learn from others who were more experienced.

Don't make the same mistake. The school of hard knocks will cost you many times more than learning from a mentor or coach. You will make so much more money by training with masters.

If you are an entrepreneur, learn to channel your free spirit, which wants to run off and do whatever it pleases. Train your entrepreneurial spirit to build a business that will bring you profits, not ruin.

My flipping business is successful because I've made the mistakes already. My system is tried and tested. It's what I do daily. It's how I conduct my business. Learning my system can help you get where you want to go.

With my Flip and Grow Rich program, which includes wealth guides and CDs, you will be able to fully capture every strategy. It will no longer be a glimpse. It's totally unlocked. Every strategy and technique I use is shown in an organized manner. These are the best strategies on the market.

**Learn from the Best**

Get an education from the best flippers in the business. This book is the beginning of your education. I have hand-picked and trained personal coaches to teach people the business. They know my system.

the bank, "You already have an exposure. This man is going into foreclosure, though he hasn't missed any payments yet." I persuaded the bank to write me the loan with no money down. It was not an assumable loan, so they wrote a brand-new loan. It was 1 percent more than the previous loan on the building.

I immediately got $260,000 in equity. The building's fully rented for $3,500 a month. So there's positive cash flow of more than $2,000 a month.

## Flipping in Other Markets

With my base in San Antonio, I plan to do deals nationally and internationally. Using the same principles and systems, I will flip houses and buy more homes in other U.S. cities because of the phenomenal opportunities available.

I also plan to acquire properties internationally, such as in Mexico and Panama. These are long-term holds, not necessarily flips. These countries promise much long-term appreciation.

As other countries become more democratic, their economies are opening to more foreign investors. These real estate markets are seeing huge upward movements, so I want to get in early and capture tremendous appreciation.

In the next several years, I will be investing on the East and West Coasts, as well as overseas. The market is ripe for the picking.

## New Mentors

Every time I venture into new markets and businesses, I continue to call on mentors. I want to learn from people who will get me

There is a reason why the best people in business and athletics have coaches. They understand the importance of having a mentor who has already done what you want to do. Why reinvent the wheel? Align yourself with people who have done what you want to do and you'll get there so much faster.

Having a real estate coach is like having a personal trainer at the gym. You walk into a gym and all the equipment is there. When you hire a personal trainer, you pay extra money and – guess what – he takes you through that exact same equipment in the gym.

But a personal trainer helps you define your goals, as well as shows you the safest and quickest ways to meet those goals. The trainer also teaches exercises that maybe you would not think of doing with the same equipment. He brings out more in you than you ever could do yourself.

A trainer helps you set goals between sessions. He suggests lifestyle changes to boost success. Most of getting in shape isn't just what happens in that one-hour training session. It's what happens during the other 23 hours of the day.

Do you really want to go back to your personal trainer or coach and say, "Guess what? All the things we talked about doing and all the goals that we set together – I didn't do any of them."

The real difference a coach makes is accountability. It's the daily actions you take that help you attain your goals. Ultimately, you can measure the results, which is how much money you have in the bank.

from point A to point Z, as quickly as possible, with as few mistakes as possible.

When I transitioned into rental and commercial properties, I again consulted my old mentors, including the doctor-investor. As I broke into new businesses – including Internet marketing, speaking and coaching – I found new mentors to guide me.

But I have strict criteria for choosing mentors. They must be the top earners in their industry. They must be the best at what they do. They must know more about their industry than I do. That allows me to humble myself before them.

I will also do whatever it takes to get educated. Early in my career, I went to an Anthony Robbins seminar. After it ended, he told us about his Mastery University, which at that time cost $10,000 for tuition. "That's a lot of money," I thought.

As we sat in the seminar, Tony proceeded to tell us the story of how he had a mentor when he was starting out. Tony was living in a car at a park then. He did not know how he would come up with money to get the training he needed. But he did. He put his money on the line.

"He did that before he was even successful," I thought. "Now look at him."

I decided to do that, too. I borrowed $10,000 to attend Anthony Robbins' Mastery University.

It takes humility to make money and a false ego is the most expensive thing in the world.

**Proven Systems**

My system is better than any other in the market. People actually see me flip houses. They know I flip houses and they know I'm a real guy. I've never met anybody who can flip more houses than I do.

A lot of people who flip houses are selling systems. They are good people with good intentions, but my system is the best on the market. I do it every day. It's not something that I used to do. It's what I do now.

My Flip and Grow Rich system was not invented 15 or 20 years ago. It is how to flip houses now. And I'm only going to work with the absolute best strategies and techniques.

The system has five parts:

1. **Foundation** - Everything you need to get started in real estate investing.

2. **Find** - Everything you need to generate leads and make deals on rehabs.

3. **Fund** - Everything you need to find money to buy your deals.

4. **Fix** - Everything you need to repair and refurbish houses.

5. **Flip** - Everything you need to sell and market a completed house.

It takes a lot to make a deal happen. My program gives you specific strategies as well as goals that you can measure and track.

## City Benefits

Since the show has aired, investors have been pouring into San Antonio, buying real estate and commercial buildings. The show has brought millions of investment dollars from all over the country. The city of San Antonio loves us and we love our city. I feel blessed to be able to give back to the city that Veronica and I call home.

The city leaders love the show. The bankers love the show. The market is hot and San Antonio will be booming for years to come.

Once you've been through your first few deals, you realize it's a lot easier than you thought.

### Serve Yourself

Many of you already have served others by raising great children, or by being a great parent, a loving wife or a caring husband. Understand that serving yourself to greater financial levels is totally OK. Give yourself permission to serve your finances. As you serve your finances, you will be able to continually serve others.

Some people serve others but never serve themselves financially. As you begin to help yourself, the number of people that you help will grow. Sometimes we need permission to serve ourselves. Hereafter, you are granted permission. Give yourself permission.

If you can't give yourself permission because you have old, negative beliefs about money, I give you permission to serve yourself, to go out and make money. All your life you have been serving, you will now be able to serve at an even greater level.

### Share the Knowledge

Take this opportunity to share what you're learning with your spouse, family or friends.

# Chapter 19

## Sharing the Knowledge
*Expanding My "Why"*

- The Need to Serve
- My Everyday System
- Future Goals
- New Dreams

### The Need to Serve

My friend Mark Victor Hansen, co-author of *Chicken Soup for the Soul*, stated it best when he said, "Flipping helps the national economy." By flipping houses, my goal and aspiration for the future is to be able to help grow people's private economies, their local economies and the overall national economy.

Originally my "why" was so that Mondo Man could know that his dad was not a financial loser. Mondo Man knows now that his dad's a financial winner.

Now, my "why" is that there are millions of people out there who need to be taught how to wise up financially and how to turn their lives around and make money. This is not good for just a few people, as they change their financial lives; it's good for the national economy.

I want to teach as many students as I can to be successful through my system, because I know it really sucks to be broke, and helping

Invite one of your friends to sit in on one of my teleconference calls. Begin to share with people what you see in this book. By doing this, you begin to build a mentality that there's more money out there or that there is enough money and we can all share it.

As you build the sharing mentality, you begin to draw a magnetic force that attracts money to you. You don't have to flip your first house to do this. You don't have to flip 100 houses to do this. You begin the sharing mentality now, by discussing this, by talking about it with others.

Understand this: You also begin to build a group of people around you who have a similar thought process. As you do this, you begin to create your own environment of empowerment. Beware of negative people. Don't allow them into your mastermind group.

Sharing is showing that you do not have a scarcity mentality when it comes to money. Rather, you have an attitude of plentitude.

**Change Your Future**

Think what flipping and learning how to flip houses through my program can do for you. Think about how it could change your life, your family name, the lives of your children and your significant other. Think about how it could change your family legacy, your lifestyle and your ability to fire your boss.

Think about how you can take more time for vacation, upgrade your car, own your dream home and earn long-term wealth

people is what gives me my greatest reward in life.

I want to touch as many lives as possible. I want to help them end their frustration and get them out of jams. This is an amazing opportunity, and I'm lucky to be able to do it.

## My Everyday System

When it was time for me to step up to the plate as a coach and mentor, it was a simple, yet daunting task.

All I had to do was take the system that I use every day and put it in a readable and understandable format. As long as I unlocked all the secrets of success of my business – not just one or two secrets – then people could learn how to succeed in real estate investing.

The personal rewards I have received are amazing, because people are so grateful. They see that what I do is real and I get letters and e-mails all the time thanking me.

## Future Goals

Michael Jordan came out of retirement because of his love for the game. I will never retire from flipping because I simply love doing it. Financially, I could retire, but my love for the game of real estate keeps me flipping.

I have flipped up to 30 houses a month. This has brought me great joy, and I want to share my knowledge. I now know that it is my mission to not only flip houses for me, but to teach others the benefits that flipping can bring their lives. It has ignited a new passion within me.

from your other properties. Think about what your life will be like when you have gained total financial freedom.

Realize that flipping can bring these to you if you do two things: make a commitment and get coached. These two actions can do everything for your life that it has done for mine.

## How You Can Learn

I have created the absolute best system on the market. When I started my career, I studied other systems. But they were always missing something. Now, I have culled the best of the techniques that do work, added strategies from my multimillionaire mentors, and combined it with my real-world business experience to bring you the most powerful and complete flipping system on the market.

I teach you my Flip and Grow Rich system through:

- workshops
- coaching
- wealth guides
- CDs
- Webinars
- teleconferences
- blogs

My teaching career is very important to me now. I teach through online seminars and my coaching company. I've made a lot of money through real estate, but being able to teach people has taken precedence over the goal of just making more money for myself.

## New Dreams

Growing up, I didn't know what I wanted to do. I knew I wanted to make money, I knew I wanted to make a difference, and I knew I wanted to be well known for doing it. But I never defined exactly what I wanted to do.

When I started flipping houses and seeing the big checks, I was hooked. That's when I knew I loved real estate.

When I got the TV show, it just fueled my fire even more. I love being on TV because I believe I have a message and a story to tell. When I go on public speaking events, it really hits me, because I'm socializing and interacting with people. I look forward to every speaking opportunity that comes my way.

I have already accomplished many of my dreams – making a lot of money, achieving fame for it, creating a legacy for my family name and helping others.

All my success comes from making an initial commitment and taking action. I did that by investing in real estate. By taking those steps, I have had every dream in my life come true. But anybody can do that.

Now my next dream is to serve. It is to serve my fans – people like you – so that you can accomplish what you want for your family, make a lot of money, make a difference in life and have your childhood dreams come true.

Step up as a student and get into the game.

Contact us at:
1-800-771-6202 x 4001 or www.armandocoaching.com

I wish you all the success that flipping has brought to my family and me!

# Acknowledgements

## Armando Montelongo

Acknowledgements are a funny thing. There are many people who have influenced my life with winning experiences as well as learning experiences. However, for this book, these are the people most relevant to the success of teaching how to get rich in real estate.

I absolutely, positively must thank my gorgeous wife, Veronica. She is my life partner, my biggest fan, my business associate and the one who teaches me to slow down and realize there are roses to smell. Veronica, you are my love, and this journey is fun because we do it together.

I must thank the inspiration for all of my success: my son, Mondo Man. One look at his face inspires me to move mountains. Son, you are my "why," the biggest reason for my success. My dream is to pass on my knowledge to you so that you, too, may create your own amazing life. I will forever be your biggest fan.

I want to thank my mother and father, Armando and Faye Montelongo, for their years of dedication to each other, which has kept me grounded in an ungrounded world. You taught me honesty and a great work ethic. What I do is simple compared with your accomplishment of raising eight outstanding children with love, fairness and class, while making it all look easy. I had no idea the hard work you put into parenthood until I became a parent. I love you.

I wish to thank my father-in-law Abel Rodriguez and my mother-in-law Maria Rodriguez. When I was at my weakest, you still trusted the well being of your daughter and grandson to me. Thank you for giving us a place to live and helping me put clothes on my son's back.

When it comes to the success of this book, I must thank my writer, Helen Chang. Helen, you kept me on track and focused during the craziest times of my life. Your attention to detail and patience, while translating my voice onto the pages of this book, is nothing less than outstanding. You are the third most patient woman I know, after the first two mentioned above.

I must thank the man that gave me an opportunity that no one else saw in me – Max Wiessman, Executive Producer of Departure Films. Your eye for talent is unsurpassed (just kidding!). Thank you for making a dramatic difference in the lives of me and my family. You have had the most profound effect on my business life. Thank you. I also thank Andrew Meyers, the first producer we ever worked with, who taught me the business of television. You are a great friend and talented producer.

I also thank the A&E network and their executives for allowing me to be true to who I am and document my life for a national audience. I hope my show has been as beneficial to you as the opportunity you have given me. Thank you!

I must thank Jeff Spangler and Cris Cannon who run my coaching company. Together, we have formulated the best real estate coaching program on the market. Thank you, Jeff and Cris, for believing in me before I was a household name. Your professionalism and friendship make this business fun. The sky is truly the limit for our partnership.

Special thanks goes to Joe Appleton who worked hand in hand with me on producing this book and my entire coaching program. It is not often I find someone who will take all of my late-night phone calls and weekend brainstorms in stride. You have been huge in coaching me on how to create and organize my educational system for growing my teaching business.

There are moments that completely change your life, and those moments have been coming toward me at light speed. One of those moments was when Michael Grow made the phone call that put in motion the events that have made my coaching program possible today. Thank you, Michael, for that very important day.

My real estate coaches and strategists also deserve a big thank you. You have been invaluable in helping me spread my message of real estate wealth to people nationwide, who so strongly desire to create the life of their dreams. Thank you for being my voice.

There are no words for how I think of this next person, my Internet manager (and guru) Joel Therien. Joel, you were a friend when I needed one most. If nothing else came from my television show, your friendship alone would have been worth it. You are one of the few people I know who shares my passion for success and the success of others. You have my undying respect.

I wish to thank Mark Victor Hansen for his input and multimillion-dollar book-selling wisdom.

There are other very important people I would like to thank: my sister, Pamela, for her years of dedication and hard work for my companies. Although she prefers that I don't mention her, her loyalty cannot go unmentioned. Pam, I love you. I am also grateful to: Mike Filsaime and Tom Beal, for helping and consulting with me for my online business;  my media lawyer, Jodi Cleesattle; my mentors, who wish to remain in the shadows, but grin at my success; and my cast mates – in particular, Randy Burch – who is my friend and keeps me laughing during our grueling shooting hours.

Most importantly, I want to thank you – the students and fans. Without you, there would not have been the public demand for me to release my real estate secrets. Without you, there would be no No. 1- rated real estate television show. Without you, I would not have experienced the best part of me. To my tens of thousands of students and my millions of fans, thank you.

## Helen Kaiao Chang

Thank you, thank you, thank you to Joe Appleton and Armando for the opportunity to work on this incredible project.

I am also grateful to my editorial associates for their professionalism, precision and friendship: Anne Wayman, Lynn McDaniel, Don Chareunsy, Jessica Farmer and Paula Pisani. Thanks also to David Bracken for his support. The design team – including Brett Gee, Debra Hunsaker, Robyn Funk and Erik DeWaal – is awesome.

Finally, my deepest gratitude goes to Wendy Suen and Robert Akong for their unwavering love and support. Thank you for enriching my life.

# About the Authors

## Armando Montelongo

Armando Montelongo is America's most notorious real estate investor. He has one of the hottest track records for fixing and selling houses – flipping as many as 30 houses a month. He was a multimillionaire by age 34.

Armando is also the star of A&E's "Flip This House" reality show, which is seen by millions of viewers each week. He is known for his straight-up, no-nonsense negotiation style – making the show the most highly-rated of its genre. He was dubbed by Entertainment Weekly as "the guy we love to hate."

Based in San Antonio, Armando is married to Veronica, the beautiful, sales-savvy co-star of the show. They have one son Armando, also known as "Mondo Man."

He can be reached at www.armandocoaching.com or 1-800-771-6202 x 4001.

## Helen Kaiao Chang

Helen Kaiao Chang is an editor, journalist and writer specializing in business, motivational and lifestyle topics. Her work has appeared in MSNBC.com, *BusinessWeek, Time, San Diego Business Journal* and many other publications. She has collaborated on two books on real estate investing. She can be reached at www.oceancloudmedia.com.

# Index

## A

A&E  230, 244, 250, 268, 304, 307
accomplishment  247, 303
analysis paralysis  59, 66
animal odors  189
ask questions  97
assessing repairs  184
assets list  63, 65, 82, 84
attorney  106, 108, 110, 111, 112, 113, 154, 267
auction  19, 148, 150, 155, 156, 161

## B

bad credit  55, 87, 155, 163
Bank of America  163
binding agreement  103
blogs  45, 299
books  20, 28, 30, 47, 86, 118, 180, 213, 245, 307
Branson, Richard  126
breach of contract  111
budget sheet  95
Buffet, Warren  35, 126
business checkup  243
business experience  15, 23, 53, 55, 299
business partners  24, 269, 271

## C

capital gains taxes  251, 253
C-Corp  265
CDs  47, 213, 289, 299
charitable donations  35
Clason, George S.  225
closing costs  81, 255, 259
Closing Loans Checklist  149
coaching  12, 16, 20, 45, 197, 199, 211, 213, 292, 299, 300, 304, 305
coaching company  16, 20, 300, 304
coaching team  45, 211
commission  159, 182, 191, 284
compassion  52, 89

competition 21, 250
competitor 194, 243
construction 15, 34, 57, 103, 107, 139
construction experience 15, 34, 57
contractual penalties 186
conventional bank 152, 163, 255
conventional bank loans 152, 163
conventional lender 255
cookie-cutter methods 192
corporation 6, 202, 251, 265, 267
county records 93, 96
courses 20, 45
CPA 16, 253, 267
credit partners 271
critical moment 59, 61, 68

# D

deadlines 18, 106, 185, 186
deals
  Before Money 85
  Expert Witness Deal 102, 110
  Fishing Guy's Retreat 192, 208
  House with Goats and Sheep 192, 194
  Multi-House Package 192, 204
  No-Mold Short Sale 192, 198
  Rancho Montelongo 248, 264
delays 118
depreciation breaks 216
divorce 123, 165, 269, 280
double close 98, 167
down payment 98, 145, 155, 163, 196, 261, 263, 266

# E

e-books 20
economies 30, 83, 290, 296
education 19, 35, 36, 45, 47, 49, 55, 71, 83, 118, 126, 146, 204, 241, 289
emotional investment 91, 109
entrepreneur 60, 180, 221, 223, 287, 289
exit strategies 153, 155, 156, 157, 171
expert witness 107, 108, 113, 115, 121, 123

# F

fear of failure  23
federal employee taxes  180
fees
  agent  196
  junk  152
  loan  152
  origination  152
  penalty  185
Five Levels of Earning Income  215, 221
Flip and Grow Rich program  103, 149, 211, 289
"Flip This House" reality show  307
foreign investors  290
Four Ds  89
full market value  114, 281
funding deals  149
future cash  277

# G

Gates, Bill  126, 176
general contractor  99, 112
global economy  83

# H

Hansen, Mark Victor  296, 305
hard-money lenders  124, 143, 206, 225, 242, 253, 280
helping people  74, 211, 273, 296
Hill, Napoleon  126
hiring employees  178, 191
holding costs  81, 141
honesty  28, 29, 31, 303
hotel fees  111
humility  132, 144, 292

# I

inner intelligence  49, 51, 59, 61, 66
inspiration  1, 38, 50, 63, 130, 213, 228, 254, 303
insurance claims  106, 109, 112, 123
insurance lawyers  91, 123, 135
integrity  27, 29, 31, 275
interest rates  17, 21, 103, 143
investment career  43
investments  17, 217, 218, 219, 223, 279

# J

jury trial  113

# K

knowledge  1, 23, 47, 144, 245, 298, 303

# L

landlords  153, 155, 167, 281
learning curve  39, 71
lease application  169
lease options  153, 156, 165, 169
legacy  9, 63, 172, 175, 199, 297, 300
legal entities  251
legal tax deductions  265
Lender Applications  149
liabilities  65, 82, 84, 100
lien  120, 122, 133, 147
loan points  152
local economy  285
long-term wealth  132, 134, 136, 277, 288, 297
lottery  23, 47

# M

managing contractors  127, 162, 166, 180, 184
market 73
  cold  81
  depressed  21
  falling  75
  fast  21, 81
  flat  81
  hot  21, 77
marketing systems  169
mastermind group  126, 176, 297
maximize profits  183, 195
Money, Meaning and Choices Institute  47
monthly payments  124, 196, 255, 263, 266
mortgage
  balance  119
  brokers  37, 152
  interest  259
  loans  127
  note  196
  principal  259
motivated sellers  73, 79, 86, 88, 89, 91, 106, 107, 127, 129, 135, 141
multimillionaire  1, 2, 132, 134, 206, 299, 307
myths  55, 240

# N

national economy  296
negative people  32, 297
negative thoughts  41
negotiation  91, 97, 101, 206, 236, 256, 307
no money, no credit  23, 45, 53
note buyer  163, 196
now cash  275, 277, 279

# O

obstacles  15, 17, 20, 61, 78
offer amount  97, 131
other people's money,  124
overhead  124, 138, 141
owner financing  150, 152, 156, 159, 163, 196

# P

peace of mind  31, 217
positive beliefs  31
positive peer pressure  43, 128
potential buyers  33, 89, 138, 152, 167, 169
pre-foreclosures  135
Private Investor Agreements  149
private investors  17, 147, 280
product lists  188, 192
product shopping lists  195
profit regeneration  221, 223, 225, 227, 277, 279, 283
project management  184, 186, 187
project manager  16, 18, 20, 154, 156, 184, 188
property
  assessment 123, 137
  manager  16
  taxes  97, 127, 259, 261
  value  75, 167, 285
prospecting  285
purchase package  93

# R

real estate agents  14, 16, 37, 91, 131, 133, 150, 153, 159, 182, 191
  rising  81
  slow  15, 21, 159
real estate contract  93, 103
real estate flipping machine  8
real estate goals  241
real-estate owned  131
recession  30, 65, 81, 83
rental agreement  169

rental houses  167, 275
research  133, 188
return on investment  124
rewards  285, 298
*Richest Man in Babylon*  225
Robbins, Anthony  126, 292
rolling economies  30

# S

70 Percent Rule  97, 99, 101, 124, 137, 141, 143, 145, 253, 283, 285
schedules  118, 177
self-employment  225
self-help books  47
self-improvement  28, 47
selling strategies  73, 153, 156, 157
seminars  20, 47, 213, 270, 300
Seven Rules to Maximize Profits  181, 183
sharing mentality  297
shopping lists  186, 195
short sale  77, 93, 131, 200
signs  150, 171, 174
slow economy  75
smart work  33, 127
Speed of Cash Theory  132, 138
standard letters  135
subcontractor agreement  57
Subcontractor Agreement  195
Subcontractor Invoicing Letter  195
supply and demand  167
support system  45
systems
  business  176
  filing  186
  finding  135
  Flip and Grow Rich  125, 135, 169, 195, 197, 293
  funding  149
  marketing  169
  paperwork  186, 191
  selling  169

# T

tax base  251, 261, 265
tax benefits  216, 261
tax deductible  220, 255
taxes  97, 127, 180, 210, 216, 218, 251, 253, 255, 256, 259, 261, 263, 265, 267
  filing  186
teleconference  297
testimony  115
*Think and Grow Rich*  126
title company  98, 139, 186, 188, 228
Trump, Donald  126, 269

# U

underinsured  90, 92, 104, 109, 222
unemployment  62, 170, 225

# V

vacations  9, 177, 190, 218, 220, 228, 233, 265
voicemail  171

# W

Webinars  20, 299
Web sites  45
Wells Fargo  163
wholesaling  153, 155
workbooks  45
work ethic  243, 303
working trips  220
workshops  213, 273, 299

## Armando's Step-by-Step Guide to Finding Investment Properties Workbooks and CDs

### Volume One

Everything you need to get started in real estate investing, so you can move on to riches: concepts, beliefs, tools.

### Volume Two

Everything you need to generate leads and make deals on rehab investments, so you can make your profit when you buy: concepts, methods, tools.

### Volume Three

Everything you need to find money to buy your deals, so you can acquire properties: concepts, methods, tools.

### Volume Four

Everything you need to repair and refurbish houses, so you can control costs: concepts, methods, tools.

### Volume Five

Everything you need to sell and market a completed house, so you can realize your riches: concepts, methods, tools.

## Order Now:
## 1·800·845·8219
## www.armandocoaching.com

## FLIP AND GROW RICH
### ARMANDO MONTELONGO
#### FOUNDATION · FIND · FUND · FIX · FLIP

# Train with Mentors with Armando's **Flip and Grow Rich Coaching Program**

Complete Coaching Program

Armando's Step-by-Step Guide to Finding Investment Properties With Coaches, Workbooks and CDs

The system is easy to learn and use. Anyone can do it. And if you want the extra coaching to enhance your skills, our coaches are here to support you.

Our coaches walk you through your deals, step-by-step, so that you have the confidence to move forward. You have an experienced team of backing you up.

The school of hard knocks can cost you tens of thousands of dollars! Don't make that mistake!

Armando's coaches can earn you tens of thousands of dollars! Learn from the best!

Create your environment of empowerment to maintain a positive investment mindset. Raise the possibilities in your life!

# Jumpstart
# Your Training
# with Armando's
# Flip and Grow Rich
# Workshops

Armando's Step-by-Step Guide to Finding Investment
Properties with a bootcamp, coaches, workbooks and CDs

Train with the best!

Armando explains his wealth-making system in a high-energy,
high-learning environment.

Gain insider tips you won't find elsewhere. Work with successful
coaches. Expand your knowledge and confidence.

Meet other investors like you, who can become part of your
environment of empowerment.

Leave the weekend ready to make massive money through
real estate!

**Call: 1-800-771-6202 x 4001**
**www.armandocoaching.com**